We Called This Creek
Traveller's Rest

BY THE DISCOVERY WRITERS

With a Foreword by Dale A. Burk

We Called This Creek Traveller's Rest...

BY THE DISCOVERY WRITERS

With a Foreword by Dale A. Burk

Library of Congress Control Number: 2003106082

ISBN 1-931291-32-2 (Softcover)
ISBN 1-931291-33-0 (Hardcover)

Published in The United States of America

First Edition

STONEYDALE PRESS PUBLISHING COMPANY
523 Main Street • P.O. Box 188
Stevensville, Montana 59870
Phone: 406-777-2729

DEDICATION

This book is dedicated to Pat and Ernie Deschamps who because of their love for Montana, its history, its people and the land, supported the efforts to save the Travelers' Rest Site.

Without their vision, patience and cooperation the site may very well have been lost forever as a public treasure held in trust for the American people of all generations. We extend our gratitude, along with that of many others, to the Deschamps for their part in preserving this national treasure.

ACKNOWLEDGMENTS

To the many individuals, family friends and colleagues, who have assisted us with this book by listening, directing, and supporting us with their expertise, knowledge and patience, we are grateful. Thank you.

First and foremost to our editor, Dale Burk, for his enthusiasm, encouragement and endless patience.

To Cover Artist: Robert Morgan.

To George Knapp and Chuck Sundstrom of the Travelers' Rest Chapter of the Lewis and Clark Heritage Trail Foundation..

And to:

Loren Flynn, Director of the Travelers' Rest State Park.

Archeologists Dan Hall, Carolynn Merrel, Jeff Fee, and Robin Johnston.

Pat and Ernie Deschamps,

Gerald Tucker,

Mary Burk,

Veto LaSalle

Jay Pinney

Scott Sproull

Rick Hurst

Kenneth Lyons

Jim Rodgers

Patty Thomas and staff of the North Valley Library, Stevensville.

Staff at the Ravalli County Historical Museum.

Staff at Missoula Public Library.

Staff at Mansfield Library with special appreciation to Christopher Mullin.

Historians and others:

Dan Peterson

John Axline

Bud Moore

Dan Peterson Research, L&C Trail Heritage Foundation

Joni Packard and staff, USFS District Ranger, Powell

Margaret Gorski, USFS, The Lewis and Clark Bicentennial Commission
coordinator.

Staff at Lolo National Forest Headquarters

Staff at Clearwater National Forest Headquarters

Tom Turner and Jean Bishop for patent search

John and Darlene Grove

Jodi Hunt

Last, but so important, the patient support of Ed Hastings, John Winthrop, Jack O'Neill, Bart Ladd and Pat Burk.

TABLE OF CONTENTS

Dedication 5
Acknowledgments 6
Foreword 9
Prologue 13
Chapter 1
Travelers' Rest in Context 17
Chapter 2
Travelers' Rest 39
Chapter 3
Medicine and Treatment 45
The Latrine 47
Chapter 4
The Lolo Trail 51
Lewis & Clark Travel The Lolo Trail 53
Chapter 5
Notes on Nature 73
Chapter 6
The Nez Perce 93
Chapter 7
Splitting The Party 111
Chapter 8
After Lewis and Clark 117
Chapter 9
Additional Aspects of The Travelers' Rest Story 121
•Pat and Ernie Deschamps 122
•Living at Travelers' Rest 123
•The Traveling Trunk 124
•The Bitterroot Valley 126
•Celestial Readings 128
•The Sweat Lodge 134
•Horses For The Corps 136

•Culturally Peeled Trees 141
•"Army Regs" 143
•Saving The Glade Creek Campsite 147
•Missoula 149
•Bonner and Milltown 150
•Lolo Pass Visitor Center 152
•Lolo Motorway 153
•Fort Fizzle 154
•A Personal Journey 157
•Honors For Clark, York and Sacajawea 159
•The Old Dutch Lady 160
•U.S. Forest Service 161
•The CCC at Packer Meadow 162
•Looking Back 164
Chapter 10
What's Ahead 165
Appendix
Time-line 175
Bibliography 179
Glossary 183
Index 185

FOREWORD

The notion that some stories beg to be told is an interesting premise, a notion that isn't always borne out by various dimensions of the story itself. And yet, some stories not only beg but demand to be told, to bring to light the dramatic flow of history, of life set in time and place so we can relate those times to our own.

Such is the case for the story told in this book of a place known since 1805 as "Travelers' Rest," the story of a small crossroads campsite along a clear mountain stream in the mountains of western Montana that achieved notice, even fame, as the setting of not one but two encampments of the Lewis & Clark Expedition, one in September of 1805 and the other in late June and early July of 1806. It was here, after all, that the Corps of Discovery camped and rested up and equipped themselves sufficiently to enable the Expedition to, first, cross the mighty Bitterroot Mountains, barely, on their trip westward and then, secondly, to complete arrangements for splitting the party for exploration jaunts on their return trip to the Marias River north of the great falls of the Missouri (Lewis) and the Yellowstone River region (Clark).

The difficulty in telling the story of Travelers' Rest, as you will learn from a variety of its stories told in this book, is not one of overcoming insignificance or vacuity. The Travelers' Rest story is a BIG story, if seen only in the context of the Lewis & Clark Expedition itself. The reality is that while the name of the place refers to the specific context of the Corps of Discovery and the time(s) it spent there, the Travelers' Rest story is much, much bigger than that – and the five ladies who constitute The Discovery Writers, already the authors of two well-received books on the Lewis & Clark theme, make sure you know that. For example, they illuminate the campsite's significance over many centuries for the Native Americans who traveled the Lolo Trail plus those which intersect with it at this precise spot and, in the process, camped along Lolo Creek at the place we now know as Travelers' Rest. As The Discovery Writers point out, Captain Meriwether Lewis may have given the spot the name that has stuck for this marvelously beautiful glen along Lolo Creek, the historic truth is that long before and long after the Expedition encamped there the site was a significant gathering place and campsite for the Salish, the Nez Perce, the Shoshone, and others.

They also tell you of the almost miraculous dimension of the story that most of the ground that constitutes the actual campsite, in the midst of a community built alongside and around and, to a bit of a degree, over it, remains undeveloped, natural, incredibly akin in shape, in flora and fauna to the time two hundred years ago when Captain Lewis remarked of this stream they camped next to that it was *a fine bould clear runing stream.* And they describe in detail the equally miraculous presence of individuals who realized that they held a priceless component of American history in their hands, the story within a story of people who did something to retain and preserve that part of our history for all succeeding generations of Americans.

To a large degree the history of Travelers' Rest over time has been one of neglect and even outright misguidedness. Out-of-sight, out-of-mind is an apt description. The authors describe, for example, how serious, professional historians misidentified the actual location of the place called Travelers' Rest – actually put into the history books and on signs telling thousands of tourists, and, I assume, history buffs like me that the site was at the confluence of Lolo Creek and the Bitterroot River when actually it was a mile and a half upstream, along Lolo Creek. Happily, the authors herein explain how that historic error got corrected, proven, a historic misadventure turned right that bears direct relationship to the fact that roughly eighty miles to the south of Travelers' Rest almost the same situation exists with the general misunderstanding that, when coming northward out of the North Fork of the Salmon River over the Bitterroot Mountains into the Camp Creek drainage at the headwaters of the Bitterroot River the party came over a spot now called Lost Trail Pass when, in fact, they did not – they crossed the Bitterroot Mountains some three-quarters of a mile to a mile to the west. Indeed, given the conditions of that crossing it's unlikely that any member of the Expedition ever set foot on the place known as Lost Trail Pass.

Some historical truths are easier to get at than the Lost Trail Pass myth, however, and the serendipity of the Travelers' Rest story lies in, as our authors tell us, of a combination of several individuals reading the journals of the Expedition more carefully and then employing common sense and the application of new technology and scientific skills of modern times. The result is, as The Discovery Writers point out, that even as we read this book new dimensions of the story are unfolding, being revealed – and therein, for us, lies the magic of the Travelers' Rest story. It is a story as old as time itself. It is a story precisely as old as the Lewis & Clark Expedition itself. And it is a story as new and exciting as last week, this week, next week .... it is an ongoing story, our story, our physical and emotional link with history, and within these pages you'll find enough components of that story, past and present, to engage yourself in a wonderful journey of your own, a journey in which you'll discover why travelers to this place before Lewis & Clark, and since, have found it a place of rest....and intrigue.

Dale A. Burk
Stevensville, Montana
April 29, 2003

COVER PAINTING

Our cover painting was done especially for this publication by noted artist R.F. Morgan of Helena under the title "We Called This Stream Traveller's Rest." It is one of many paintings Mr. Morgan has done on the theme of the Lewis and Clark Expedition. In this particular painting, Captains William Clark and Meriwether Lewis are depicted at a site overlooking the place of encampment along Lolo Creek. The snow-covered hills and "awesome mountains" to the west that the Expedition had to cross on their journey to the Pacific Ocean loom in the background of the scene.

PROLOGUE

September, 1805

Thomas Jefferson sighed, candlelight flickered over the map on his desk, illuminating the signature, "William Clark". Ah, yes, William, an outstanding frontiersman, soldier and cartographer. What a fortunate choice Meriwether made in selecting William to partner with him on the long mission he, Jefferson, had engineered; a scientific exploring expedition across the vast American continent to the Pacific Ocean. Surely, these two young men will find new plants and animals, as yet unknown, meet the native tribes and persuade them of the peaceful intentions we, in Washington, have for them. Ah, and should they locate that evasive Northwest Passage, the United States would be one up on the British. We know the expedition survived last winter at that remote Mandan Indian Village, for here on my desk is the very map William made which Meriwether sent back with his reports and plant and animal specimens, a live bird, the magpie, and the little rodent, the prairie dog. All had arrived safely. But that was April, and it is now September. Where is the Expedition now?

Jefferson rose from his desk and strolled out onto the balcony. Fireflies lit up the grounds below him, a horse neighed in the darkness, and garden flowers sent soft fragrances into the warm September night. A faint pink aura etched the horizon and drew Jefferson's imagination westward into that unknown land, *"the terra incognita"* and he pondered aloud "Are they still alive?"

A clock chimed the hour stirring the President from his reverie. Candlelight pooled around his desk. Carefully, he returned Clark's map to its place on the shelf and blew out the candle.

September 9, 1805

Captain Meriwether Lewis shivered in the cold air of the high mountain valley where he and the members of the Expedition, the Corps of Discovery, as President Jefferson had named it, camped beside a clear mountain stream coming in from the west which "*we called Traveller's Rest.*" Light faded across the meadow, shadows lengthened and flickered over the campfire. A young Indian mother crooned a lullaby to her suckling baby while horses grazed on rich grasses. The captain glanced around with the eye of the experienced army officer, determined that the camp was in good order and scanned the towering mountain range ahead. He sighed and bent over his journal, "*those unknown formidable snow clad Mountains.*" The Corps of Discovery was about to embark on the most perilous period of its journey to the Pacific, along a faint Indian trail blocked by fallen trees and thick brush, into mountains where snow was deepening, food was scarce and winter was already blowing its icy breath.

Embers showered from the campfire and landed near the captain's feet. He rose, stamped them out, and looked over his shoulder toward the east. Many miles away, long miles away – President Thomas Jefferson was waiting, anxious to hear their stories, anxious for their safe return with news of the Northwest Passage which Meriwether Lewis would have to tell him did not exist. He turned toward his tent. Tomorrow! Tomorrow they would take on those mountains.

September, 2002

Rain arrived today, a stranger, welcome to Montana in the waning weeks of a very dry summer. The Bitterroot River is alarmingly low as is the little tributary flowing in from the west, Lolo Creek, once named Traveller's Rest Creek by members of the Lewis and Clark Expedition. On the banks of both the river and the little creek a small community, Lolo, is thriving. History has defined this area as the campsite of the Lewis and Clark Expedition when it journeyed west in September, 1805 and returned in June of 1806. This night shadows lengthen across the valley and lights, like fireflies, pinpoint the ranches farms and homes that are scattered between the Sapphire and Bitterroot Mountain ranges. The aroma of barbecue drifts across neighbors' fences, and a horse neighs from a nearby pasture.

The Travelers' Rest chapter of the Lewis and Clark Trail Heritage Foundation is meeting in the Lolo Community Hall. Lights shine from the windows, the door opens on the hum of excited voices. An important discovery has been made, important to these students and enthusiasts of the famed Corps of Discovery. Their interest and enthusiasm for the Lewis and Clark Expedition is shared and fanned by members of the Heritage Foundation across the continent. After years of speculation, the exact spot where the Corps camped here has been located – to the precise spot – by modern technology and archeological digs. Travelers' Rest now joins Pompey's Pillar, also in Montana, as the only two places on the Lewis and Clark Trail where physical evidence actually verifies the presence of the Lewis and Clark Expedition. Also, the Expedition camped here twice, in September of 1805 and July of 1806. What does it mean? Jubilation fills the hall as members voice possibilities for preservation, for education, for the Native Americans to speak, for expansion, for signs and publicity for commercial benefits. Chapter president Chuck Sundstrom strikes his gavel, opening the program......

Darkness descends quickly in the mountains. The meeting concludes, someone switches off the lights while members straggle out to their vehicles to return home, some to the south along Hwy. 93 in the Bitterroot Valley, some north and east to nearby Missoula and its vicinity. Others turn west over Hwy. 12, past Travelers' Rest toward " *those unknown formidable, snow clad Mountains*" along a "northwest passage" unimaginable to those early 19th century travelers who crossed those same mountains on horseback two hundred years ago.

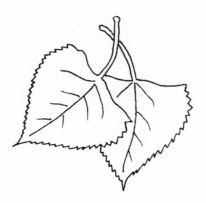

An aerial photograph of the Travelers' Rest site (marked with a ★ on the photo) taken in July of 1937 shows a landscape, along Lolo Creek at least, surprisingly akin to what Lewis and Clark might have encountered. While there is modest agricultural development in the area, very little of the housing development that now surrounds the area had taken place. The Bitterroot River is at the right, Lolo Creek flows from left to right, and both U.S. 93 running north and south and U.S. 12 east and west along the flank of a totally undeveloped Lolo Hill. North is at the top of the photo. Photo courtesy Jay W. Pinney. (See photo on page 38, also.)

Chapter 1

TRAVELERS' REST IN CONTEXT

Mystery, intrigue, drama, romance, suspense and adventure illuminate that great American epic, the Lewis and Clark Expedition, as written in the journals of the captains and men of the Corps of Discovery. Thomas Jefferson, third president of the United States, had already sent out two previous expeditions designed to explore the western territory of the American continent. Both had failed. Yet the Expedition, led by Captains Meriwether Lewis and William Clark, did succeed and still intrigues and stirs the imaginations of historians and scholars, scientists and archeologists, writers, readers and common citizens. Two hundred years have passed, yet books continue to appear detailing every aspect of that journey; the travelogue, the observations, the travails, the personalities, the Native Americans, the campsites.

One such campsite is Travelers' Rest, a site wrapped in the folds of the Bitterroot Mountains of western Montana and bordered by Lolo Creek. Here, the Corps of Discovery rested in September 1805 and again in the summer of 1806 during their intrepid journey to the Pacific Ocean and back. In these mountains this little band of men, one teen-age Indian mother with babe, their horses and a stout-hearted dog struggled against all that nature could hurl against them – and won.

Since ancient times Native Americans have stopped at this campsite when traveling east across the great Divide to hunt buffalo, when journeying west over the rugged mountains to the rich fishing waters of the Columbia Basin or when trekking south through the Bitterroot Valley to trade and socialize with other tribes. Travelers' Rest was the hub of these Indian trails, the crossroads where for centuries "the people" intermingled and intermarried, traded, hunted, celebrated together. They filled the creek side with the sound and spirit of their voices, shouting, singing, praying, dancing, exchanging stories and possibly defending themselves against their enemies. Indian blood, sweat and tears had already enriched the soil here when the Expedition arrived. But the white men named this place, and wrote it into history through the context of the Lewis and Clark Expedition.

Long subservient to the "importance" of more prominent Expedition sites, Travelers' Rest was generally described by a misleading highway sign as being at the mouth of Lolo Creek where it empties into the Bitterroot River. However, when the exact location of the campsite of September 9-11, 1805, and June 30-July 3, 1806, was determined by scientific means and archeological digs in 2002, Travelers' Rest was propelled into prominence as one of only two sites where actual physical evidence verifies the Expedition's presence. The other, also in Montana, is the signature of "*Captain Wm. Clark, 1806*" at Pompey's Pillar.

How did this field of memories remain untouched for nearly two hundred years while growth and development pressed in on all sides? How was this long buried secret unveiled? Who were the people involved? What are the plans for the future of this historic site? For the Native Americans stories? For the heritage rooted here and for the community of Lolo?

The story begins in the fertile mind and imagination of Thomas Jefferson who by his diplomatic skill, political savvy, and sharp intelligence engineered and brought this Expedition to fruition under the leadership of his young secretary, Meriwether Lewis, and Lewis' friend, William Clark. When Jefferson was given the opportunity to acquire the vast territory west of the Mississippi River to the Continental Divide, he managed through diplomatic intrigue to sidestep the Constitution and purchase Louisiana from France. Thus, the Expedition was assured of traveling through United States territory.

From the day the captains launched their little flotilla onto the Missouri River on May 14, 1804, their aim was to reach that point at which they would find the waters of the Columbia River, which they presumed would take them to their destination, the Pacific Ocean. Their understanding and their hope was to realize a short and not too difficult portage from the headwaters of the Missouri over the Continental Divide, to where they could float their canoes down the waterways to the Columbia. The little fleet labored up the Missouri to the Mandan villages in North Dakota where they built Fort Mandan and passed the winter of 1804-1805. When the ice broke on the river, the Corps continued their journey up the Missouri struggling against the current under grueling circumstances, bearing with extremes of weather, illness, mosquitoes, prickly pear cacti and unexpected challenges from wild buffalo and grizzly bears. Finally, the travelers reached the Great Falls of the Missouri. To their dismay, the portage there, which they expected to be no more than a day and a half, took a month of grinding labor, and they were still far from the headwaters of the Missouri and the mountains. Furthermore, they had met no Indians.

Their journey continued up the river, passed through the Gates of the Mountains and to the Three Forks of the Missouri. There the little band rested for two days before they pushed up the river coming in from the west, the one they named Jefferson after the President. While Captain Clark piloted the canoes up the narrowing river, Captain Lewis walked ahead with three men in search of Sacajawea's tribe, the Shoshone Indians, which, she assured them, summered here. Lewis was desperate to find the Indians who had horses crucial to the Expedition if it was to cross the mountains before winter. Finally, on August 13, the Shoshone did appear after Lewis had peacefully encountered a Shoshone woman and two girls. Out of the brush sixty Indian warriors galloped at full speed toward the captain and the three soldiers, a scene worthy of a Hollywood western. In an act of bravery, coupled with desperation, Captain Lewis dropped his gun, held up the American flag and approached the warriors indicating peace. It worked. The Indians accepted his good intentions, and their Chief Cameahwait escorted him back to their camp. In an unforgettable moment in history, and an unimaginable scenario, Sacajawea recognized Cameahwait, the chief, as her brother.

From these poor destitute but proud relatives of Sacajawea the captains learned that there was a trail to the north, the "road to the buffalo" used by the Nez Perce Indians to cross the mountains. It was difficult but passable. Could the Shoshone have also indicated a well-known campsite connecting the trails? The hungry Shoshone were on their way to hunt buffalo, but although their people were starving, they delayed to assist the white strangers and trade horses. In return the captains left considerable trade goods, agreed to send traders who would exchange guns and ammunition for their furs and promised peace from their new great father in Washington. The Shoshone turned east to the Big Hole Valley and the buffalo; the Corps of Discovery traveled north toward those tremendous, snowy mountains that blocked their path to the Columbia.

'Those Emmence Mountains'

A veil of mystery still lingers over the Bitterroot Mountain Range as to exactly where the Corps of Discovery crossed over that twisted maze of mountains from the North Fork of the Salmon River in Idaho to the valley of the Bitterroot River in Montana. Chief Cameahwait and Old Toby, their newly acquired Shoshone guide, pleaded with the captains to go back the way they had come over the Lemhi and to the Big Hole. Then, the Indians advised, follow 'The Road to the Missouri' (Nee Mee Poo Indian trail) to where another trail intersects coming up from "the big clearing" (Ross Hole) through the pass (Gibbons Pass). This is a longer but easier route to the valley. The Expedition leaders, however, chose not to follow this advice but proceeded to force their way through these mountains. But the Bitterroot Mountains are brutal, cold, and rugged. They would introduce themselves to the members of the Expedition like a giant throwing down the gauntlet and challenging the little band to cross over. President Jefferson's detachment would need all the strength and resources it possessed to meet that challenge.

Scholars of the Expedition do not agree as to the exact route over this range of the Bitterroots which now divides Idaho from Montana. The late Dr. Gene Swanzey, an acknowledged authority on the Lewis and Clark Expedition, however, is adamant:

"The people, who for generations used the area encompassed by the pass the most, didn't name it anything – they knew where it could lead them. The Corps of Discovery never did get near what is now called Lost Trail Pass. Most likely Old Toby implied a 'no way' and the hunters spread out, desperately seeking game, and surely reported back to the party...Lost Trail Pass is a nice name except there was no trail to get lost."– Swanzey, Eugene, (Discovery Writers, *Lewis and Clark in the Bitterroot*, p. 28)

Journals of the Expedition are illuminating in their own right. For example, on September 2, 1805:

"we passed through verry bad thickets where we were obliged to cut a road for our horses to pass through...steep along the edge of the mountains and very rough and rockey...this is a very lonesome place... we call this place dismal Swamp...some of our weak horses fell backward...we had considerable of trouble this day carrying several of the horses loads up the steep rockey mont." – Sergeant Ordway.

The travelers were passing over steep talus slopes where sharp rocks cut the feet of their shoe-less horses, and Sergeant Gass noted that York's feet were so sore he had to ride horseback.

September 3, 1805: *"hills high and rockey on each Side...so Steep that the horses could Scur[ce[ly keep from Slipping down...Several sliped & Injured themselves verry much... but little to eat...we passed over emmence hill and Some of the worst roads that ever horses passed...our last Th[er]mometer broken, by accident...Snow about 2 inches deep."* – Captain Clark

Here the journals grow confusing. Temperatures were still being recorded on September 4 and 5, also there are errors in Captain Clark's bearings.

September 4, 1805: *"the morning clear but very cold. Our mockersons froze hard.. The mountains covered with Snow...set out and assended a mountain without anything to eat...our fingers aked with cold."*

Dr. Gene Swanzey: *" On the morning of September 4, once thawed out, they angled back below the highest point of Saddle Mountain to a low spot of the ridge line and descended to the dividing ridge between the East and West Forks of Camp Creek."*

At Camp Creek: September 4 to September 6, 1805

When the exhausted band and their bruised and battered horses wound

The majestic Bitterroot Range as seen from the Bitterroot Valley in western Montana, a snow-covered obstacle to the Expedition on both its outward bound and return journeys.

their way down to the valley, they encountered the *Oot-la-shoots*, a band of Tushapa Indians, members of the Salish or Flathead tribe, at a meadow the Indians called *"the great clearing."* This is Ross' Hole near Sula, Montana. Indian oral tradition relates that the strangers had been observed by the band's scouts who reported to their chiefs that a strange, bedraggled-looking party of men were straggling toward their camp. They had skin like ashes and wore no blankets. Perhaps they had been attacked by enemies who had stolen their blankets. One man was painted black, the sign of a war party. However, a woman and baby traveled with them. Surely, a war party would not have a woman with baby. Fortunately for the Expedition, the Indians, who could easily have killed them and stolen their guns and provisions and had discussed doing such a thing, instead *"rec[e[ved us friendly, threw white robes over our Sholders & Smoked in the pipes of peace,   we Encamped with them & found them friendly, The Chief harrangued untill late at night, Smoked in our pipe and appeared Satisfied…. "had 33 Lodges, about 80 men 400 Total and at least 500 horses."* – Captain Clark.

Another key comment from the journals: *"and they look like tolerable good horses, the most of them."* – Sergeant Ordway.

On September 5, 1805, Patrick Gass wrote that there was a *"great white frost. The Indian dogs are so hungry and ravenous that they eat 4or5 pairs of our moccasons last night."*

 The Expedition faced a critical need, fresh horses to replace the worn bruised and battered Shoshone horses. When the captains attempted to describe this need to the chiefs, the interpretation passed through five languages. The captains spoke English to Labiche, who converted to French for Charbonneau, who translated into Hidatsa for Sacajawea, who passed the message to a young Shoshone lad who spoke in Salish to the Oot-la-shoots, all probably aided by sign-talker, George Drouillard. However clumsy the translations, the Expedition *"did purchase 11 horses & exchanged 7 for which we gave a few articles of merchandise, those people possess ellegant horses."* – Captain Clark.

September 6, 1805. The Salish, like the Shoshone, were hungry and anxious to hunt buffalo. The white travelers were eager to continue journeying westward. They said good-bye. Indians rounded up their ponies and dogs and headed over the Nee me poo trail to join their Shoshone neighbors. Those hospitable Salish! Did they suspect that without their help and their horses, these strangers would probably have perished on their next encounter with those *"turrible mountains."*? Many years later one of their chiefs, Charlot, would lament, *"We were happy when he, (the white man) first*

Horses obtained from both the Shoshone and the Salish to use as riding and packing stock, as well as a source of food on several occasions, were of major benefit to the travelers. Photo courtesy Tina Giaimo.

came from the light; but he comes like the dusk of evening now, not like the dawn of morning. He comes like a day that has passed, and night enters our future with him." (Ronda, p. 255)

The Land of The Red Willow

Time to travel north through the land of the red willow (the Bitterroot) where the Indians had assured them that the Nez Perce trail to the buffalo was just four nights journey north. Again the journals read *"a clear cold morning,... rained this evening...northing to eate but berries, our flour out and but little Corn..."* Captain Clark

To men who were used to eating eight to nine pounds of meat a day, rations were slim. Finally the hunters were able to bring in two deer and the next day an elk which brought smiles and good humor to the travelers. *"Our party seemed revived at the success that the hunters had met with, however in all the hardship that they had yet undergone they never once complained, trusting to Providence the Conduct of our Officers in all our difficulties."* – Joseph Whitehouse.

Their course down the valley followed the river known to the Indians as "*spe'tlemen*" meaning "place of the bitterroot" or in Salish "*spitlem seukm*" or "water of the bitterroot." Lewis named it "Clark's River," and later it was known as the Flathead. In 1898 the U.S. Forest Service gave its official name "Bitterroot". The valley opened out now and offered better forage for the horses. Traveling proved easier, but the snowy crag-crowned mountains on the left haunted the thoughts of the journalists:

Snow top mountains to our left." – Clark.

"*Some of the highest are covered thick with snow.*" – Joseph Whitehouse.

"*The snow continues on the Mont. Each side of this valley..Mountains of snow back on our left.*" – Sergeant Ordway.

Old Toby persuaded the captains to cross the river for easier traveling, and they proceeded down the east side over stony land. Bruised feet, turned ankles and thorns from the prickly pear cactus troubled the men, horses, and "our dog, Seaman."

September 8, 1805: The campsite was south of Stevensville in a field described by Whitehouse as having "*fine feed* "for the horses and where the hunters brought in an elk and a buck. Dr. Swanzey claims that the Corps followed the current route of the Eastside Highway fairly closely, and they probably trudged right down the route that is now the main street of Stevensville, which was a favorite Indian camp and dance ground.

September 9, 1805: After breakfasting "*on a scant proportion of meat which we had reserved from the hunt of yesterday*" the travelers continued to follow the river which Clark described as "*a handsome stream about 100 yards wide and affords a considerable quantity of very clear water, the banks are low and its bed entirely gravel. The stream appears navigable...but no salmon in it...there must be a considerable fall in it below.*"

Old Toby did not know where this river entered the Columbia, but he did inform the captains that there was an overland route to the east that would take only four days to reach what Lewis determined was the vicinity of the gates of the mountains. Four days? And they had traveled 55. After midday dining the party crossed the river in water "*very cold and up to our horses' bellies.*" The travelers proceeded north on the west side along an Indian trail, and, finally, reached a small clear creek coming in from the west which they called "*Traveller's Rest.*"

The Campsite

For decades a Montana historic highway marker mistakenly read "The Lewis & Clark Expedition...camped at the mouth of Lo Lo Creek." However, when the little band turned west and moved along the creek the captains halted at a field about one-fourth to one-half mile above the mouth of Lolo Creek

September 9, 1805: *"as our guide informs that we should leave the river at this place and the weather appearing settled and fair I determined to halt the next day rest our horses and take some scelestial Observations. We called this Creek Travellers rest...a fine bould clear runing stream."* – Captain Lewis

September 10, 1805 : Hunters departed to bring in provisions for the trip ahead while Captain Clark explored the Bitterroot River to its junction with the river flowing in from the east, which they tentatively called "Valley Plain River," then settled for "the East Fork of the Clark River" (DeVoto, *Course of Empire* p. 503) This is present day Clark Fork River which flows through Missoula, Montana. Meanwhile, a frightening surprise awaited hunter John Colter this day, when three Indians suddenly appeared out of the trees..

"On first meeting him the Indians were alarmed and prepared for battle with their bows and arrows, but he soon relieved their fears by laying down his gun and advancing toward them." – Captain Lewis.

This drawing by Gustav Sohon titled "Entrance to the Bitterroot Mountains. By the Lou Lou Fork" is believed to be the earliest known visual presentation of the site that is known as "Travelers' Rest." The campsite was along the timbered creek at the far right of the picture, now the setting of the community of Lolo, Montana. See Page 104 for more information. Courtesy K. Ross Toole Archives, University of Montana.

Fortunately, Colter returned riding on the back of an Indian's horse. These Nez Perce Indians, who were mistakenly identified as Flatheads, claimed to be chasing some Snake (Shoshone) Indians who had stolen their horses. They brought good news to Captain Lewis, however. They had crossed over the terrible mountains and had relatives who lived on the other side, on the Columbia River where water was good and capable of navigation. Also, some of their relatives had traveled to the sea where they met an old bearded white man who had given them handkerchiefs like those of the Expedition. The Indians told Captain Lewis that the trip over the mountains *"would require five sleeps."*

Time to rest, to dry out and mend clothing and moccasins, to tune up and repair guns and other equipment and to store up food. The captains took observations, caught up on their journals while the others steeled themselves for their next excursion into the formidable mountains.

Over the "Road to the Buffalo"

September 11 to September 22, 1805: Some horses strayed and caused a delay but at 3 p.m. the Corps of Discovery moved west along Lolo Creek girding themselves for the encounter with those stupendous mountains

The Travelers' Rest campsite circa September of 2002. Courtesy Travelers' Rest Heritage and Preservation Association.

which had already proven *"fatiguing almost beyond description"* as written by Sergeant Gass. This journey proved to be longer and worse.

"The road was excessively dangerous along this creek being a narrow rocky path generally on the side of steep precipice...if either man or horse were precipitated could inevitably be dashed to pieces." – Captain Lewis.

"The men are becoming lean and debilitated, on account of the scarcity, and poor quality of the provisions on which we subsist; our horses feet are also becoming very sore." – Patrick Gass.

Captain Clark, that hardened soldier and frontiersman admitted, *"I have been wet and cold in every part as I was in all my life, indeed I was at one time fearful my feet would freeze in the thin mockersons which I wore."*

The Indians were right. There was no game and no forage for the horses. Old Toby missed the trail and brought them down to the fishing weirs he remembered, a delay the travelers could not afford. The strenuous climb back up the mountains to Wendover Ridge was exhausting to both men and horses. These brave ones fought the cold, killed three horses to keep from starving, grew weaker and sicker and kept on going. Men wrapped rags around their feet to keep from freezing. On September 18, Captain Clark took six hunters and went ahead in search of food and in the hope of meeting the Nez Perce. They found a stray horse, killed it and left food hanging for their starving comrades. On September 20, they met the Nez Perce, who supplied them with salmon and camas which they sent back to their companions.

September 22, 1805: Finally, the bedraggled band of men, Sacajawea and baby, horses and dog, dragged themselves onto Weippe prairie, home of a band of Nez Perce Indians. All were afflicted with open infected sores, and weakened from malnutrition and dysentery caused from the unaccustomed food. The Indians could easily have killed the vulnerable strangers and stolen their weapons and supplies. Instead, Native Americans once again saved the Expedition.

Two and a half weeks passed before the Corps of Discovery could continue their journey. Slowly, the members regained their strength, branded their horses, which the Indians had agreed to keep until their return, and managed to construct five dugout canoes.

Journey to the Ocean

October 7, 1805: The travelers left their Nez Perce hosts and lowered their cumbersome canoes into the Clearwater River. The first day they had to ride nine rapids. The journals are filled with death-defying exploits over the rapids, of canoes being tossed about and broken up, of portaging and of dangerous escapes from drowning and death. In late October at the Dalles, the Indians gathered on the shore to watch the white men drown. Stephen Ambrose notes, *"By the standards of today's canoeists, this was a Class V rapid, meaning it could not be run even in a modern canoe specially designed for white water."* (p. 306) But these intrepid travelers and skilled watermen surprised the doubting and eager Indians waiting to salvage their equipment. They rode the rapids without incident.

Unlike their trip up the Missouri where they met no Native Americans, these Indians lined the river banks. Two Nez Pierce chiefs, Twisted Hair and Tetoharsky, traveled with the Americans to warn of rapids ahead and to prepare the Indians in advance of the white men. On October 9, 1805, Old Toby and his son left unexpectedly without a good-bye and without pay. Not being river men they were probably frightened by the dangers of river travel and wished to return to the safety of the mountains. The Indians remained agreeable which Captain Clark, on October 13, 1805, attributed to the presence of Sacajawea which, *"we find reconsiles all the Indians as to our friendly intentions...a woman with a party of men is a token of peace."*

Captain Clark also noted the culinary habits of the river Indians who enjoyed roasted dog which Captain Clark could not stomach and Captain Lewis found quite tasty. On October 16, 1805, the party embarked onto the Columbia River. The two Nez Perce chiefs, fearing the enmity of the Indians downriver, now said good-bye and returned home.

Time was important; get to the coast in case a trading ship may be there. Hurry to settle in camp before winter sets in. The supply of trade goods was now dwindling, much of it lost in the canoe mishaps or spent for supplies. Although language was a barrier the captains made every effort to be friendly to the Indians they met, presenting them with medals, speaking of peace, of trade goods and of their new white father in Washington. Cruzatte entertained with his fiddle and York danced. However, when the Indians pilfered from them or stole important items like a tomahawk or Drouillard's capote, the captains and men demanded a return. Fortunately, tense situations managed to be resolved.

The terrain grew rocky and inhospitable. For ten days bad storms pinned the party down while rain and river water drenched their tents and rotted their leather clothes. When the Corps finally reached the ocean a decision had to be made as to where to locate their winter camp. November 27, 1805: the choice of a campsite was put to a vote by the captains. Everyone voted including, for the first time, a woman, Sacajawea, who was a Native American, and a black man, the slave York. It was a day notable in United States history.

"Janey (Sacajawea's nickname) in favor of a place where there is plenty of Potas." (probably roots) – Captain Clark.

Elk were more abundant on the south (Oregon) side where scouts found a suitable place for winter quarters. Here the men constructed a log stockade, Fort Clatsop, named for their Indian neighbors, where they wintered from December 7, 1805, to March 23, 1806. Out of 141 days there it rained all but twelve. Captain Clark described the Pacific Ocean: It *"roars as a repeaeted roaring thunder and have rored in that way ever since our arrival in its borders...I can't say Pasific as since I have seen it, it has been the reverse."*

Spelling

Why is the spelling and grammar written in the Journals of the Lewis and Clark Expedition inconsistent and varied? From 1783 through 1785 Noah Webster published a three-part "Grammatical Institute of the English Language" that helped start to standardize spelling. But – the first actual dictionary, "Compendious Dictionary" was not published until 1806; and the "American Dictionary of the English Language," was issued in 1812. The familiar "American Dictionary of the English Language" which has been revised many times came out in 1828. The Journals were written before a standardized spelling was being taught and used. Most members of the Expedition were uneducated or poorly educated frontiersmen, except for Captain Meriwether Lewis. Noted historian and writer Bernard DeVoto maintained that "The spellings of the original are a large part of its charm." (DeVoto, Journals of Lewis and Clark, p. xv.)

Christmas dinner consisted of spoiled elk meat and rotten fish. Still the men and Sacajawea kept busy repairing tools and guns, constructing clothes and moccasins from the elk skins, drying jerky, and making salt. They hunted, traded, mingled with the local Indians and welcomed their neighbor, Clatsop Chief Coboway, who brought gifts of food to their camp. The writers wrote in their journals, sketched and constructed maps while all members of the Corps tried to cope with the constant dampness, injuries, colds diseases and fleas. They never met up with a trade ship as they had hoped. And there was no Northwest waterway connecting the two great oceans.

Still Captain Lewis wrote, March 22, 1806:

"Altho' we have not fared sumptuously this winter at Fort Clatsop, we have lived quite as comfortably as we had any reason to expect we should; and have accomplished every object which induced our remaining at this place."

Return From The Ocean

March 23, 1806: Time to return home, and the Corps of Discovery was in a hurry. Time was essential if they were to collect their horses from the Nez Perce before the Indians moved from their winter camp and to get over those terrible Bitterroots and on to the Missouri before it iced up. Also, the captains had made an important decision while at Fort Clatsop, and they were eager to put into effect. They would split the party at Travelers' Rest. Meanwhile, the captains must continue to promote and encourage intertribal peace with the Indians, and survive with what little trade goods remained. These endeavors would require all the patience, grit, determination and skill the captains and their men could muster.

The river Indians had already been in touch with white traders and had learned to drive a hard bargain. Also, they were starving, had little food to trade, and would pilfer anything that was left unguarded. Tense and dangerous conflicts resulted, and at times the men of the Corps were pushed

This drawing from the 1880s depicts the Hot Springs at the source of Lolo (Lou Lou) Creek. Compare it with a scene on the opposite page taken at the site in 2002.

to the edge and were ready to kill. Three Indians stole Seaman, and Captain Lewis, in a rage, sent men to rescue his Newfoundland *"and shoot if necessary."* The frightened Indians dropped Seaman, and no shots were fired. Patrick Gass observed that there were *"honest Indians from Rocky Mountains to the falls of the Columbia, from the falls west they are all rascales and thieves."*

Fortunately, no man fired his gun at any Indian, nor did they burn any homes.

The river, in flood stage and very dangerous, challenged the skilled boatman and the strong men pulling and tugging over rapids. Multitudes of curious Indians looked on from the banks and some threw stones down upon the struggling men. Finally at the Dalles, they left the river, purchased horses and marched overland where on April 27, 1806, the Walla Walla Indians and Chief Yellipp welcomed them with food and celebration and indicated a shortcut which eliminated eighty miles. Once again they joined their friends, the Nez Perce, who returned the horses. By now the party was desperate for trade goods. Fortunately, Captain Clark had the reputation of being a medicine man, and through his ministrations he was able to barter for food. Even the brass buttons from their coats were used for trade. On May 7, 1806, the travelers saw their nemesis in the distance, the snow-covered Bitterroots. The Indians warned, however, the snow was too deep. WAIT. After three weeks of waiting and frustration, impatience and

anxiety, the Corps ignored the advice of the Indians and started over the trail without a guide. The mountains almost won this one when on June 16 the snowdrifts were twelve to fifteen feet high, and the order was given to turn back, the only retrograde march of the entire journey. When the Nez Perce deemed it safe, they provided young men to guide their white friends over the trail. Crossing the mountains this time was still difficult and dangerous, but took only six days to cover 160 miles as compared to eleven days the year before. Finally, on June 29 the weary party arrived at the spot where the present-day Lolo Hot Springs is located, a welcome opportunity to sooth their aching bodies. Then on to Travelers' Rest.

Travelers' Rest: June 30 to July 3, 1806

The hunters, finding ample game, supplied the weary travelers with tasty and nourishing dining. The Bitterroot Valley bloomed with rich grasses for the horses, and provided Captain Lewis the opportunity to discover and describe the "bitterroot" in late but full bloom. Here, the . captains completed their plan to divide the party and proceed with their explorations. On July 3, the camp broke up, the Captains bid good-bye and turned their parties in opposite directions, Captain Clark traveled south up the Bitterroot Valley; Captain Lewis proceeded north and then east along the "*road to the buffalo.*" The men and Sacajawea by now had bonded into a community and must have felt some apprehension as to the fate awaiting them. Would they ever see one another again? They would be traveling in dangerous territory without the support of the full company. But with good cheer and trust in their captains, they followed them. James Fazio states, "*the separation would be for 40 days with many of those days presenting challenges of death-defying proportions would end with what seems like the clearest evidence of all that Divine intervention can be the only explanation for the amazing success of the Lewis and Clark Expedition.*" (p. 185)

The Indian guides, though fearful for their friends, the "Shalees," (Salish) and eager to return home did linger long enough to guide Lewis and his party to the "*road to the buffalo*" which would lead them across the Divide to the Great Falls of the Missouri.

Lewis with nine men, Gass, Drouillard, the Fields brothers, Werner, Thompson, Goodrich and McNeal, seventeen horses, and the five Nez Perce guides proceeded along the Clark River (Bitterroot) past the junction with the Hellgate River (today's Clark Fork) to where the guides pointed out a place to cross. There the men constructed three rafts from scarce timber in the vicinity, while the Indians swam their horses and drew their baggage in little *"basons"* of deer skin followed by the Expedition's horses. Captain Lewis and two men who were weak swimmers were the last to cross on a raft which had been drawn about one and some half miles downstream. An overhanging branch knocked Lewis into the swift current where he barely escaped being swept away, but he made the river bank safely as did the two men. They camped that night near the Grant Creek juncture west of today's Missoula, where the mosquitoes tortured them, their horses and Seaman.

July 4, 1806: Although Captain Lewis tried to persuade the Nez Perce guides to travel with his party to the Great Falls of the Missouri, they refused, indicating that the travelers no longer needed guides as *"the road to the buffalo"* was so well traveled that even white men couldn't miss it. They wanted to look for their Shalee relatives and were also afraid of the Pahkis, their enemies, (the Minnatarees) whom they warned Lewis might *"cut them off."* They smoked a farewell pipe together then parted, a sad parting for good friends who had camped, ate, slept, played and crossed the dangerous mountains together. The Corps of Discovery owed much to these young Native Americans who now returned down the Clark River (Bitterroot) in search of their relatives, from which Captain Lewis concluded

A photo taken in the 1890s shows an Indian encampment on the plain to the west of what was known as Hell Gate Canyon. The city of Missoula, Montana, now covers this entire plain.

there was not a good route by land along the river *"by which we came"* to the plains of the Columbia.

As the men and horses marched along the north side of the river, they passed through the area where the city of Missoula now stands, probably along a route about where present-day Broadway is located and across the river from the University of Montana. The mountains closed in on a canyon (Hellgate) which cut through to a prairie and on to the juncture with today's big Blackfoot River, known as the *Cokahlahishkit, or* the Nez Perce *"River of the Road to Buffalo,"* which they described as sixty yards wide rapid and deep. Following their guides instructions, Lewis turned his party east along the north side of the river which is hemmed in by heavy timber and high rocky mountains. Where they camped, they noted, there were no mosquitoes.

Homeward Bound

July 7, 1806: Lewis and his men crossed *"the dividing ridge between the waters of the Columbia and Missouri rivers"* over what is now known as Lewis and Clark Pass, although Clark never saw it. One easy step and the men were once again in the United States where they viewed the Great Plains and salivated for the buffalo meat they knew was there. Six days later, the travelers reached their destination, the White Bear portage camp of 1805, opened their cache in anticipation and found, instead, that high flood water had destroyed much of their treasure. Another disappointment.

On July 19, 1806, Sergeant Ordway and his crew of nine men arrived at the White Bear portage camp after being dispatched down river by Captain Clark from the Three Forks of the Missouri. Here they were to assist Sergeant Gass and his crew in portaging the Great Falls. The captains' plan then called for both parties to continue down river and join Captain Lewis and his men who would be returning from their exploration of the Marias River.

In high spirits the little flotilla proceeded down the Missouri to their rendezvous with Captain Clark and the rest of the Expedition. They met on the Missouri River near the mouth of the Yellowstone on August 12, 1806. What joy when all the members of this little community, the Corps of Discovery, found each other well and accounted for, well, except for Captain Lewis who had been inadvertently shot in the buttocks by one-eyed Pierre Cruzatte who had mistaken him for an elk. The wound was nowhere near mortal, but the captain was so miserable and indisposed that the duties of leader, diplomat, doctor and journalist fell to Captain Clark.

At Two Medicine

Captain Lewis left camp July 16, 1806, with Drouillard and the two Fields Brothers in the hope of finding that the Marias River watershed would lead above the 49ᵗʰ parallel to the Saskatchewan River in Canada. After exploring for six days, however, a disappointed Captain Lewis wrote, "I now have lost all hope of the waters of this river ever extending to N latitude 50 degrees."

The little party was now on Cut Bank Creek where the captain decided to stop and camp, rest the horses and take observations. But the weather turned disagreeable, cloud cover prevented his taking observations, and a frustrated Captain Lewis wrote, "adieu to this place which I now call Camp Disappointment."

The four men hoped to avoid meeting any Indians, nevertheless, on their return at Two Medicine, several young Piegan Blackfeet appeared. Lewis opted for diplomacy and invited the young Indians to camp with them. While they smoked together, the captain endeavored to give his peace and trade message through sign language. However, at "first light" the Indians attempted to steal the mens' rifles and horses. In the fracas that subsequently occurred two Blackfeet were killed. This was the only fatal encounter between the Expedition and Native Americans throughout the Expedition's twenty-eight month journey. Now Captain Lewis and his men had to ride for their lives, and they did covering 120 miles in less than twenty-four hours. In another scene, again worthy of Hollywood, these four riders reached the Missouri, heard rifle shots, looked upstream and saw their own men approaching. With great haste they unsaddled the horses, jumped into the canoes and were off. Could their timing have been more perfect? Incredible luck or Divine Providence?

With Clark On The Yellowstone

Captain Clark and his party turned south from Travelers' Rest, passed through the Bitterroot Valley, across the Nee Mee Poo Trail that they had dismissed the year before and into the Big Hole Valley. At Camp Fortunate, now under the waters of Clark Canyon Reservoir, the men opened their cache from the previous year, retrieved the specimens and canoes and then reveled in the tobacco they had buried there. The travelers continued by canoe and horseback to the Three Forks of the Missouri where Captain Clark split the party according to plan and dispatched Sergeant Ordway and nine men in six canoes down the river to the portage site at the Great Falls of the Missouri. Here, in her homeland, Sacajawea directed Captain Clark to a pass she knew, present-day Bozeman Pass. For this Captain Clark commended her: *"the Indian woman has been of great service to me as a pilot through this country."*

July 15, 1805, the little band reached the *Rochejhone River* (the Yellowstone) at present-day Livingston. An interesting note from Captain Clark reads: *"Two of the horses was so lame owing to their feet being worn quit smooth and to the quick...I had moccersons made of green Bufflow Skin..which Seams to relieve them very much."*.

When Private Gibson's horse threw him, he was so severally injured he could not ride. His companions constructed two canoes, lashed them together and the little company proceeded by canoe and on horseback. By now the Expedition had empty pockets. All their trade goods were gone except the horse herd which must have been a welcome sight to those accomplished horse thieves of the Plains, the Crow Indians. When half the horses were missing Captain Clark directed Sergeant Pryor and three men to herd the remaining horses overland to the Mandan villages where they could be traded for food. The second night out the remaining horses disappeared. The four men were now stranded, but with the skill and resourcefulness of frontiersmen, they backtracked to the river, killed buffalo and made two Indian bull boats from the hides. They then proceeded down the Rochejhone (the Yellowstone) hoping that they could catch up with Captain Clark. Nevertheless, on August 8, 1806, in another happy twist of fate, Pryor and his party arrived whooping it up when they recognized Captain Clark and their companions .

July 25, 1806. The travelers arrived at a sandstone outcropping, which Captain Clark climbed and named Pompey's Tower after "Pomp," little Jean Baptiste Charbonneau. He then carved the memorable inscription *"Wm. Clark, July 25, 1806"*. The journey continued. At one point huge *"gangues"* of buffalo blocked the river. The men couldn't sleep listening to thousands of beaver slapping their tails, mosquitoes were so thick that Captain remarked he could not sight his rifle because of those pesky *musquetors*. They met no more Indians, food was easily available, and the river mostly navigable. They met trappers traveling upriver already on their way to the beaver fields. The future of the American West was about to be laid open.

August 12, 1806: The rendezvous was complete; the Corps of Discovery united, and the Lewis and Clark Expedition was on its way home.

The Return to St. Louis

Two days later they were once again at the Mandan villages. Here, the Charbonneau family left the party after agreeing to travel to St. Louis the following year and bring little Jean Baptiste to Captain Clark, who had promised to rear and educate him. John Colter asked for and received permission to leave the Corps and return upriver, back to the fur fields. The remaining crew traveled easily down river with the current. They met traders going upriver who supplied them with news and whiskey, and who, in turn gathered information about those vast western lands and the beaver waiting to be trapped, about the Indians who inhabited the land, about grizzly bears and buffalo, and about the great Columbia River and the Pacific Ocean. They passed by the Teton Sioux but refused to stop, paid their respects and filled in the grave of Sergeant Charles Floyd, their comrade who had died the previous year. On September 23, 1806, the men arrived at St. Louis at *"12 oClock amidst cheers from the crowdes gathered on the riverbank."* They had been gone two years and five months and covered over seven thousand miles.

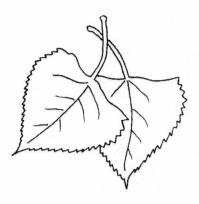

By August of 1955, the date this aerial photograph was taken of the Travelers' Rest site (marked with a ★ on the photo) at Lolo, there had been hardly any more development in the area than was the case in the 1930's. Today, most of the Lolo area, including the bare hill at the lower center of the picture, is covered with homes. The Bitterroot River is at the right, Lolo Creek flows from left to right, and both U.S. 93 and U.S. 12 show clearly. North is at the top of the photo. Photo courtesy Jay W. Pinney.

Chapter 2

TRAVELERS' REST

Meeting the Salish in September of 1805 at what is today called Ross' Hole, near Sula, Montana, gave the Lewis and Clark Expedition opportunity to gather fresh horses, gain information about the journey ahead, and trade gifts and political talk. After saying goodbye, the men of the Expedition continued their passage through the rain-chilled Bitterroot Valley and intersected a long-used, old Indian crossroad, the Buffalo Road. (The Lolo Trail today follows it fairly closely.) The old Indian trail connected the east to the west and gave passage through the Bitterroot Mountains. For the Salish, Nez Percé, the Coastal Indians, the Blackfeet, Kootenai, Shoshone, Pend d'Orielle, and others, it *was* The Northwest Passage. Hopefully, it would lead the Expedition across the mountains into Idaho, and onto a water-passage to the Pacific Coast. Captains Lewis and Clark, heeding the advice of their Shoshone guide, Old Toby, chose a place to rest themselves and their horses, repair and prepare their guns and gear, and hunt for as much wild game as possible to pack for the mountain crossing. They named their rest camp "Travellers rest."

On September 9, 1805, Meriwether Lewis wrote that the party had *"encamped on a large creek which falls in on the west. As our guide inform[ed] me that we should leave the river at this place and the weather appearing settled and fair I determined to halt the next day rest our horses and take some celestial observations. We called this creek Travellers rest. It is about twenty yards wide, a fine bold clear running stream. The land through which we passed is but indifferent, a cold white gravely soil. We estimate our journey of this day at nineteen miles."*

On their return in the early summer of 1806, they once again stopped to rest and reconnoiter, and to finalize plans for a divided party with separate missions. (They were to join again on the Missouri River later.) Captain William Clark, on June 30, 1806, wrote *"...a little before sunset we arrived at our old encampment into Clarks river a little above its enterance into Clarks river. Here we encamped with a view to remain two days in order to rest ourselves and horses and make our final arrangements for separation."*

Modern Times

Travelers' Rest is now a National Historic Site and a state park. It was listed on the register of National Historic Landmarks by the United States Department of Interior, and the National Park Service, and given a bronze plaque that was issued in 1964. The distinction carries benefits: consideration for Federal grants; limited protection by Advisory Council on matters relating to historic properties; and certain tax recoveries and reforms. The designation honors both the Landmark and the individuals and organizations that have worked to preserve it.

Unfortunately, the site originally designated as "Travelers' Rest" was not quite correct. Historians, Lewis and Clark enthusiasts and scholars could not match that site with the story told, or the maps, in Captains Lewis and Clark's journals. Wrangling "discussions" ensued along with lengthy investigation and research.

A surveyor, cartographer, and hydrologist, Dr. Robert Bergantino at Montana Tech, University of Montana, in Butte, Montana, was asked in to help, and in 1998 published a report called, "An Evaluation of Original Lewis and Clark Information to Determine the Location of Travelers Rest Camp, Lolo, Montana." The monograph identified Travelers' Rest Camp as being west of U.S. Highway 93, not east; and almost two miles upstream from the confluence of Lolo Creek and the Bitterroot River, which was outside the boundary of the National Historic Landmark designation given to the old site. Bergantino stated, *"We know that Travelers' Rest Camp was not at the mouth of Lolo Creek. We have good evidence that the campsite was near the Indian road the Expedition followed September 9, 1805, which, in all likelihood, approximated the present alignment of U.S. 93 and Clark's field map and his Atlas Map 69 show Travelers Rest Camp west of the Indian road a short distance."*

Preservation

The summer of the year 2000, archeological research was funded for the newly identified site of Travelers' Rest, and the U.S. Forest Service and Montana Community Development Corporation awarded funding toward the site acquisition and operations. The burgeoning population of the Bitterroot Valley put increasing demands on housing, and residential development was fast encroaching upon the Travelers' Rest site. In 1999 it was listed as one of eleven most endangered historic places in the United States.

Fortunately, a philanthropist's purchase of a four- acre plot, which was rolling toward development, preserved a portion of the campsite. The following spring fifteen acres were purchased and donated to the State of Montana for the site of a State Park. Two additional ten-acre parcels were later incorporated. (One of them was a local philanthropic donation, from local residents Bill and Ramona Holt, for an easement or a trail. It appeared future generations would have the legacy of the campsite, and it would also be treasured, enjoyed and made to good use by the community and the public at large in time present. (The acquisitions were possible because of benefactors, interested individuals, the Mellon Foundation, The Conservation Fund, Montana Department of Fish Wildlife and Parks, and the Montana Community Development Corporation.)

In 2002, archeologist Dan Hall and his crew began excavation at the Travelers' Rest site, and using procedures and equipment such as metal detection, Magnetometer, EM 31, Mercury Vaporizer, Aerial Infra-Red Photography and others the crew unearthed the Expedition's latrine, and evidence of a cook-fire. Mercury found in the latrine's bottom was inestimably significant. Both Captains Lewis and Clark used it for medical treatment to doctor the men of the Expedition.

Additionally important, the depth of the latrine fit the prescribed military regulation of eighteen inches, plus the fire-pit was also at the military's prescribed distance of three-hundred feet from the site of the latrine. The accumulated evidence for the site was probably influential in identifying Travelers' Rest as one of two most nationally significant sites in Montana by the Montana Lewis and Clark Bicentennial Commission. (The other site is Pompey's Pillar near Billings, Montana.) The campsite of Travelers' Rest is one of the few places on the Expedition's trail where there is objective, material, confirmation of their historical passage.

The Park

Travelers' Rest Preservation and Heritage Association was incorporated in 2001. It is a nonprofit organization that manages public land; and being responsible for the Park, its interpretation and protection rests on the Association's shoulders. TRPHA, as it is called, is trusted with the activities, programs, and conservation of Travelers' Rest Park. The Park has many layers of history and culture and TRPHA has chosen four points of interest: 1. The importance of the site to Native American tribes – the Nez Percé, Salish, Shoshone, and others; 2. Travelers' Rest as a pivotal site for the Lewis and Clark Expedition; 3. The account of the Homesteaders who cut out a life for themselves in the Bitterroot Valley; and 4. The landscape's geology, botany, biology, and natural history.

The projected plans to carry out these themes are to be through interpretive and interactive programs. (Self-guided or interpreted trail hikes, and live demonstrations.) The projected design also includes using fewer buildings and exhibits, and to put to use the campsite's natural environment and character. It will be an on-going process. If Captain Clark could see this place today, might he exclaim, *"Oh, The Joy!!"*

Buttresses

Many individuals and organizations worked to preserve the historic Travelers' Rest campsite. Among the first was the Travelers' Rest Chapter of the Lewis and Clark Trail Heritage Foundation, which formed in 1987 after a series of lectures and field trips. Professor Harry Fritz, (University of Montana, History Department) proposed a local Chapter could be valuable for people in the area interested in Lewis and Clark. The Chapter remains active today presenting interesting public speakers, lectures, and field trips relevant to the broad range of themes and viewpoints of the Expedition and their trail. They also promote fundraising projects from which they are enabled to contribute and benefit other Lewis and Clark sites and projects. One of the Chapter's projects has been "The Traveling Trunk," a footlocker that contains replicas of articles carried on the Expedition that are shown along with demonstration and informative explanations. According to 2003 statistics, 26,000 people have seen, enjoyed, and learned many facts about the Lewis and Clark journey across the nation.

Some of the Chapter's members, at the time unconvinced of the accuracy of the designated location of the Travelers' Rest campsite, initiated the search for a more credible and verifiable site documented from the journals of Captains Lewis and Clark. They sought-out surveyor, Dr. Robert Bergantino, for assistance, thereby taking the first step in preserving the legacy of that important site.

The identification and preservation of the campsite was possible because of the effort and generosity of many groups and individuals. Some of the organizations, services, grants, and bureaus have already been mentioned, so this will be a further listing: The Community of Lolo, The Conservation Fund, Missoula County Office of Planning and Grants, Montana Department of Fish, Wildlife and Parks, Montana Community Development Corporation, University of Montana O'Connor Center for the Rocky Mountain West, Montana Community Foundation, VIAs Multimedia Productions, HUD, Cost Share, and Montana State Representatives. As the U.S. Department of Interior says, the preservation of historic landmarks honors both the landmark and individuals and organizations that worked to preserve it.

Travelers' Rest still sits along the crossroads of travel and commerce. Now, however, it is a Park, and emblematic of the rich heritage of three different cultures or experiences – the Homesteaders, American Indian tribes, and the Lewis and Clark Expedition's passage.

The precise location of the Travelers' Rest campsite and preservation of it were hard-won historical victories. It took a combination of tenacious scholarship and effort, high regard for the Expedition's endeavor, and the dedication and generosity of many individuals and organizations. The old campsite Landmark expresses the legacy of the old Buffalo Road, and the Expedition of Lewis and Clark. It has endured, and will now continue, and as it does it will enrich the lives of its visitors and the residents of the Bitterroot Valley.

Dr. McDowell's mahogany chest holds the common frontier nostrums, often valued in proportion to how bitter they tasted. Most of them were used only as purgatives or emetics, but in pioneer households the cathartic Calomel, a mercury compound, doubled as an insecticide, and Squills, a stimulant, was also "a fine rat poison."

A replica of the "Medicine Chest" of Dr. Benjamin Rush similar to that which was carried on the Expedition.

Chapter 3

MEDICINE AND TREATMENT

The health of those under the command of Captain Lewis was one of the many duties for which he was responsible. During Expedition preparations, his medicine chest was supplied with the bare rudiments of treatments and medications.

At an early age Lewis had learned from his mother, Lucy, the healing properties of herbs, but Dr. Benjamin Rush was his medical advisor prior to leaving Philadelphia. Not only was Dr. Rush one of the most learned and prominent physicians of his day, he was a leader, patriot and reformer. His education consisted of private academy and the College of New Jersey. After graduating from Princeton at the age of fifteen, he had a medical apprenticeship for six years. Upon receiving a medical degree at the University of Edinburgh, Rush worked briefly in a London hospital and returned in 1769 to begin medical practice in Philadelphia. He was a friend of Thomas Jefferson, an acquaintance of Benjamin Franklin, and a signer of the Declaration of Independence.

In Rush's era, disease was thought to be caused by poisons or "morbific matter" found in the body. His simple solutions to rid the patient of these elements were bloodletting and purging the digestive tract. Purging usually consisted of a dose of his pills known as "Thunderclappers".

The Corps of Discovery suffered various diseases, discomforts and injuries, but, except in extreme circumstances did they allow themselves to stop because of them. Their mission was to forge on; they were not charged with studying the effects of disease or injury.

Most physical ailments were treated with a dose or two of Rush's pills. Some of their maladies were nausea, fever, abdominal cramps, diarrhea, sore eyes, wounds, syphilis and gonorrhea, skin eruptions, and the effects of poor diet. Rush's pills made with calomel (mercurous chloride) and the root of the jalap plant, were given freely.

It was thought that Dr. Rush had patented his pills, but a patent search by Tom Turner of the U. S. Patent Office revealed he did not. The common term "patent medicine" did not mean a medicine was patented. Nicknamed "blasting powder," Rush's "compounds cathartic" were still used by the Army in World War II; however, mercury is now considered a poison and is no longer used.

After the Corps of Discovery conquered the Bitterroot Mountains on the outward journey, the Nez Perce shared their dried salmon and root breads with the starving men. The entire party gorged themselves and soon suffered the consequences of "heaviness of the stomach and the running of the bowel." The combination of gorging and the bacteria in the dried salmon probably caused these violent results. The Indians were immune to the bacteria, as dried fish was part of their normal diet. But the effects of Rush's pills they were given to purge their systems only compounded the

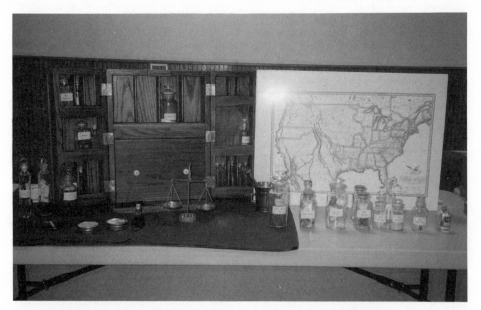

A replica of the medicine chest carried on the Lewis and Clark Expedition with its contents displayed as part of a demonstration made by the "Traveling Trunk" presentation of the Travelers' Rest Chapter of the Lewis & Clark Trail Heritage Foundation. (See item in Chapter 9.)

men's suffering, plus the dehydration that surely followed.

Venereal disease, especially syphilis, was known as *"lues venerea,"* the Latin term for sickness, disease or pestilence. The origin of the disease is still unknown, and was recognized as a dreaded disease spread by sexual contact. Although there was yet no cure, the treatment was drastic. Mercury was the drug of choice to treat the "pox," and it was administered by two different methods – given orally or as a topical ointment. Lewis also took with him penile syringes for the other venereal disease, gonorrhea.

The problem of sore eyes was caused by poor diet, wind or dust. The treatment was a solution of water, zinc sulfate and lead acetate. Measured out carefully, this acted as an astringent to contract the eye tissue and ease the pain. The Indians, who also suffered with this irritating symptom, prized this medicine. On the Corps' return journey, Clark traded the Nez Perce for needed items after treating their eyes and other maladies.

An example of injury along the trail occurred when Private Potts sustained a severe cut on his leg while crossing the mountains on the return trip in 1806. Lewis made a tourniquet and sewed the wound, which later became inflamed and painful. However, on June 27th he wrote, *"Potts leg which had been much swelled and inflamed for several days is much better this evening and give him little pain." (Thwaites 5 p.167)*

As the practice in those days was purging and bloodletting, it was a tribute to the strength of the men accompanying Lewis and Clark that they survived both the disease and the cures. By administering mercury salts in the treatment of gastro-intestinal problems and syphilis, the latrines received frequent use. Therefore, large amounts of mercury could have been found there. This fact helped archeologists to establish the location of the latrine at the Travelers' Rest campsite.

THE LATRINE

In July of 2002, Daniel Hall, historical archeologist for Western Cultural, Inc. in Missoula, theorized that the Expedition's latrine at the Travelers' Rest campsite would contain traces of mercury from Dr. Rush's Thunderbolts administered to the party as a cure-all – which were composed of 60 percent mercury. Lewis' journal entry of July 2, 1806, confirmed that both Silas Goodrich and Hugh McNeal, at that time were both *"very unwell with the pox which they contracted last winter with the Chinnook women"* and were being treated with mercury. (Thwaites 5, p.180)

The famous "sink" in which the latrine used by members of the Lewis and Clark Expedition at Travelers' Rest, which was positively identified via some sophisticated scientific sleuthing described in the text, is at the right lower corner of this photograph. Coincidentally, the site is just inside, by a few feet, the eastern edge of the park property.

In a never-tilled meadow beside Lolo Creek, Hall identified an area that appeared to have a subsurface rectangular trench. Using a piece of equipment called an EM 31, an electromagnetic instrument that passes electrical current into the soil, he looked to see if this instrument would register any anomalies, things out of the ordinary, in the ground. Surprisingly, electrical currents were detected, and since no mining activities had ever been carried out on this place, Hall's crew was prompted to begin excavating and testing the soil with a mercury vapor analyzer.

As they dug, every ten centimeters they stopped to test the soil for mercury. Multiple samples were taken at each level. The first thirty-eight samples showed negative; these upper layers were Lolo Creek gravel of rounded, unsorted cobbles. Then, below this was a diverse layer composed of a darker soil, rich in organic material and stone free – decomposed latrine earth; this soil still tested negative. At forty-eight centimeters the organic layer returned to more creek bottom deposit, but at fifty centimeters the reading on the mercury vapor analyzer read .01004 milligrams of mercury per cubic meter of soil! That is just where one would expect to find mercury, at the bottom of the latrine. Because mercury is a heavy, inert element, it does not decompose; water has difficulty flushing it away.

At this remarkable discovery, the crew filled the air with screams of delight. Even further celebrating occurred when a soil sample taken to the laboratory showed yet a higher level of mercury: 0.0145 milligrams per cubic meter of soil. Pay dirt! Archeologist Hall exclaimed, "It's about as much excitement as you can get standing over a two-hundred year old latrine!"

Since the Expedition was a military operation, it was governed by Army regulations. This included the arrangement of encampments. As for the latrine or "sink," it was to be situated three hundred feet from the camp cook fire. This sink was to be a trench twelve to eighteen inches deep. At the Travelers' Rest latrine, mercury was found at the approximate depth of nineteen inches. The distance between this latrine and the camp's cook fire *does* measure three hundred feet.

The latrine's discovery was significant for two reasons. Until then, Travelers' Rest has been listed as a National Historic Landmark that incorrectly showed the camp at the confluence of Lolo Creek and the Bitterroot River. This is about one and a half miles east from the proven location upstream on Lolo Creek. Plans are underway to petition the National Park Service this summer of 2003 to get the site designation changed to the right place. Secondly, Travelers' Rest is one of the few spots along the Expedition trail where there is decisive proof of their presence; Pompey's Pillar along the Yellowstone River in southeastern Montana is another.

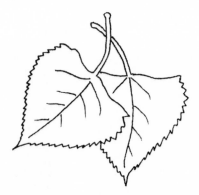

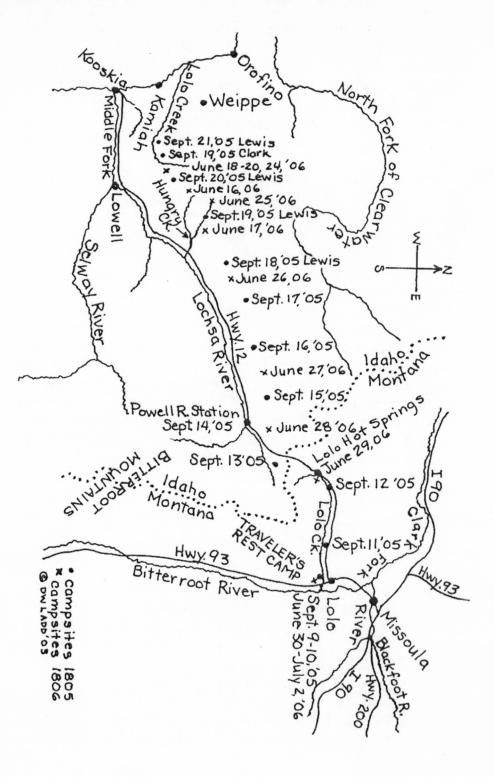

Kooskia

Orofino

Lolo Creek

Weippe

North Fork of Clearwater

Kamiah

Middle Fork

Sept. 21, '05 Lewis
• Sept. 19, '05 Clark
  June 18-20, 24, '06
• Sept. 20, '05 Lewis
× June 16, '06
  × June 25, '06
  Sept. 19, '05 Lewis
  × June 17, '06

Hungry Ck.

Lowell

Selway River

• Sept. 18, '05 Lewis
× June 26, '06

• Sept. 17, '05

W
N
S
E

Lochsa River

Hwy. 12

• Sept. 16, '05
× June 27, '06

Idaho
Montana

• Sept. 15, '05

× June 28, '06

Lolo Hot Springs
June 29, '06

Powell R. Station
Sept. 14, '05

BITTERROOT MOUNTAINS

Sept. 13 '05 •

I 90

Clark Fork

Idaho
Montana

Sept. 12 '05

TRAVELER'S REST CAMP

Lolo Ck.

Sept. 11, '05

Hwy. 93

Bitterroot River

Hwy. 93

Lolo

Sept. 9-10, '05
June 30-July 2, '06

Missoula

Blackfoot R.

I 90

Hwy. 200

• Campsites 1805
× campsites 1806
© DW LADD '03

—50—

Chapter 4

THE LOLO TRAIL

The Lolo Trail extends one hundred and sixty miles east to west from the mouth of Lolo Creek, Lolo, Montana, to the Weippe Prairie near Weippe, Idaho. It winds along creeks and rivers, through thick, tangled undergrowth, up and down steep mountainsides and along ridgetops. A canopy of thick pine, spruce and fir trees shelter most of it. Artifacts have been found linking man to this historic corridor and many places still bear evidence of hundreds, possibly thousands of years of use.

The greatest distances of the Lolo Trail follow ridgetops and roughly parallel Lolo Creek on the Montana side of the Bitterroot Mountains, and the Lochsa and Clearwater Rivers to the west in Idaho. There are high mountain meadows, bogs, alpine forests, rivers strewn with huge granite boulders, hot springs and some of the most beautiful country in the world.

It is a beautiful but dangerous landscape, especially from early September to late June. Without much warning, this pristine area can suffer the wrath of Mother Nature, which may manifests itself in the form of fierce storms of rain, sleet, snow or hail pushed by deadly cold. If trapped here for any length of time, it is easy to starve to death for there is little food. Historically, the trail was used by wild game and Native Americans thousands of years prior to white man's first visit. The Flathead, Salish, Nez Perce and possibly other tribes used it as a footpath in search of food and trade items. The Nez Perce, in north-central Idaho, traveled east of the mountains for buffalo, roots and berries. The Salish and Flathead traveled west to obtain camas roots and salmon in the Columbia River basin.

In the 1700s, the horse was introduced to the tribes of the Pacific Northwest by the Spaniards, making summer pilgrimages across the Bitterroot Range easier and more frequent. As a beast of burden, the horse transported large packs of food, pulled travois and carried riders. With the advent of the horse this age old trail, marked by peeled or blazed trees, rock cairns and familiar landmarks, was said to be the shortest distance between green meadows. Primarily an Indian road to food sources, in 1805 and 1806 it became a passage to and from the Pacific Ocean for the Lewis and Clark Expedition. In the years to follow, it served fur traders, trappers, prospectors, hunters, soldiers, recreationists, loggers, sightseers, historians, foresters and railroad surveyors as a footpath and corridor connecting them to people and places either side of the mountains. With the exception of mining and logging activity and a few recreational spots, this area has changed little in thousands of years. After the near extinction of the tremendous buffalo herds east of the mountains by the white man, the Indians had little reason to make the difficult journey. Parts of the trail overgrew with brush and were obliterated by new trails, roads and highways.

The Lolo Trail still lures people from all walks of life to its exploration

Part of the original Lolo Trail along the top of a ridge high in the mountains of Idaho. Photo courtesy Jean Clary.

and kindles a desire within each to experience a little of the adventure of two hundred years ago. Thanks to the concern of several individuals, groups and government agencies, sections of this historic trail can still be traversed. Many miles of the trail are environmentally fragile areas and in those areas officials fear that too much traffic could erase forever the traces of the Lolo Trail's history.

THE EXPEDITION TRAVELS THE LOLO TRAIL

Crossing a dividing ridge west of Lost Trail Pass and then flanking the eastern front of the Bitterroot Mountain Range, the Corps of Discovery continued to push the boundary for western expansion beyond the Louisiana Purchase westward. If the United States was to take possession of the northwest territory extending from the Continental Divide to the Pacific Ocean, it must do it quickly. This unclaimed area was sandwiched between land to the south in Spain's possession and British claims to the north. For years, prior to becoming president of the United States, Thomas Jefferson sought to explore the possibility of a trade route extending from sea to sea. Finally, his dreams had come true.

One year and four months into the Expedition, the Corps of Discovery was preparing to cross the Bitterroot mountain range to travel westward into the land of the Nez Perce and then onward to the Pacific Ocean. Weary and needing a place to rest, the party did as the Flathead, Salish, Nez Perce and possibly, other tribes had done for centuries. They stopped near the mouth of Lolo Creek to rest, plan and prepare for the difficult trek ahead.

Why the Lolo Trail? To reach the Pacific Ocean before the rivers iced over, the Lolo Trail was the most direct overland route connecting the expedition to the navigable waters of the Columbia River. " *....and all appear perfectly to have made up their minds to suceed in the expedition or purish in the attempt. We all believe that we are now about to enter on the most perilous and difficult part of our voyage, yet I see no one repining: all appear ready to met*

those difficulties which wait us with resolution and becoming fortitude."
Although these were the words of Captain Meriwether Lewis on July 4, 1805, after portaging around the great falls of the Missouri and as the Corps of Discovery prepared to enter the Rocky Mountains, they were certainly true for this part of the voyage. Having just experienced the difficult climb from the Salmon River drainage to the Bitterroot Valley and having some idea of what lay ahead, every member of the Corps was committed. Through the struggles of the Corps of Discovery came the story. With their maps and journals in hand, we can, in a small way, experience it with them.

September 11, 1805 – Delayed by the loss of horses, the Corps of Discovery left Travelers' Rest at 3:00 p.m. The sun beamed down warmly as they advanced up the wide, open road running along the north side of Lolo Creek. On this beautiful autumn day, Captain Clark could not help but notice the high snowy peaks to the south (Lolo Peak, elevation 8,692 ft.) as well as the rugged hills lining the trail's northern side. They traveled seven miles before stopping to camp at the mouth of a small stream (today's Woodman Creek) where they found an old Indian camp site. Both Sergeant Ordway and Private Whitehouse mentioned passing a pine tree where several Indian symbols were painted and from which hung a white bear skin.

This view of "those terrible mountains" across which the Expedition had to travel were covered with snow on both their journeys across them. Photo courtesy Jean Clary.

Whitehouse wrote, *"We suppose this place to be a place of Worship among them."* The first day's travel had been easy but that would soon change.

September 12, 1805 – Departing camp at 7:00 a.m., the party continued along the creek. The route became increasingly difficult. Thick undergrowth blocked their passage while downed trees and treacherous rock slides marked the hillsides. Passing another old Indian camp, they noticed an earthen sweatlodge and several peeled trees where they turned north. They continued along some steep hillsides tripping and sliding as they crossed windfall and rocky areas. The struggle lasted for twenty-three miles. They finally found a small meadow around 8:00 p.m., although for some it was more like eleven. *"We encamped on this Creek, where we had scarcely Room to lay down to Sleep,"* wrote Private Whitehouse. Located two miles east of Lolo Hot Springs near the mouth of Grave Creek, the campsite is in the vicinity of the Montana State Highway maintenance building. Captain Clark best described the day in the following quote: *"The road through this hilley Countrey is verry bad passing over hills & thro' Steep hollows, over falling timber &c. &c. continued on & passed Some most intolerable road on the Sides of Steep Stoney mountains which might be avoided by keeping up the Creek which is thickly covered with under groth & falling timber."*

Trail Section
In 2001, the Lolo National Forest purchased twelve hundred acres and an easement of two and one-half acres from Plum Creek Timber Company for 1.6 million dollars. This land deal put fourteen miles of the Lolo Trail extending from Graves Creek to Lolo Pass in public trust. (Space, p. 16)

September 13, 1805 – Given free rein to graze, Captain Lewis' horse and a colt were missing. The captain, along with four men, conducted a search, while the main party set out over a bad road. At two miles, the road merged with many trails in an area where hot water issued freely from huge granite rocks. Surrounded by a large meadow of grass and camas, this was a natural draw for humans and animals alike. The natives had blocked the largest flow with rocks and mud forming a bathing pool. Captain Clark estimated the temperature of the hottest springs was "nearly boiling." Spending just enough time to wash their faces and sample the water which they declared good with a little taste of sulfur, the party prepared to set out. Which of the many trails was the Nez Perce road? *"my guide took a wrong road and took us out rout 3 miles through intolerable rout..."* – Captain Clark.

Did Old Toby lead the party astray? Most people seem to think so. However, Private Whitehouse's journal entry clouds the picture somewhat. It states, *"We could not get along the Indian trail, for the timber that had been blown down in a thicket of Pine & other Trees - We went round a hill, and got into the road again."* Everyone was tired and frustrated, and it was easy to take it out on their Indian guide. As you will see later on, whether this or any other detour was solely Old Toby's fault is questionable. Traditionally, Indians followed the ridges while white men followed waterways. They finally hit the northern Nez Perce road (Lolo Trail) and much to Sergeant Gass' delight, the going was easy for the next four to five miles. Always looking for grass for the horses, Captain Clark halted the party in a green meadow on Lolo Creek to await the arrival of Captain Lewis' party. Shortly, they arrived without the lost horses. Immediately, two men were sent to continue the search as every horse was deemed value to the expedition's success. This part of Lolo Creek was littered with beaver dams. The prospect of getting food and especially beaver, sent every available man scrambling. Beaver tail, considered a delicacy when they were on the upper Missouri, was rivaled only by buffalo tongue as the Expedition's most sought after food. Disappointed at finding no beaver, the travelers continued along Lolo

Lolo Hot Springs

Lolo Hot Springs resort is located on the north side of U.S. Highway 12 and Lolo Creek in a beautiful setting of huge granite rocks encompassing a ten-acre meadow of grass and camas. At an altitude of 3,786 feet and approximately thirty five miles south and west of Missoula, Montana, the hot springs has enjoyed resort status for a long time. First used by the Indians for making bows, forming horn into tools and ornaments, and for medical and bathing purposes, the springs were also, a place of spiritual significance for the Indians. After Lewis and Clark and the Corps of Discovery visited, many white men came. Trappers, prospectors, settlers and recreationists from near and far made the springs a favorite stopping place. In no time, it was touted as a wonderful resort – having a hotel, cabins, a store, a saloon and eventually a post office. Its history includes many colorful and interesting stories, some of which have probably been embellished through the years but then maybe not! Today it offers all the amenities of a nice resort. There is something for everyone. For most Americans, it is of historical significance. The Lewis and Clark Expedition was here in September of 1805 and again in June of 1806.

Creek, reaching the summit of a high mountain (Wagon Mountain near Lolo Pass). Continuing, they passed the head waters of Lolo Creek, where the party had a bird's eye view of the jagged snow-covered mountains to the south/southeast. Falling on a small creek, they crossed the divide, taking them from the Bitterroot watershed in present day Montana to Idaho's Lochsa drainage. The creek escorted the party into a fifty-acre flat filled with lush grass and camas (today's Packer Meadow). For centuries, this magnificent high mountain meadow had been a special gathering place for the natives, where members from several tribes dug camas roots and stripped the inner bark from the surrounding pines. Captain Lewis called the meadow Quamash (Indian word for camas) or Camas Glade.

Packer Meadow
Today, Quamash Glade is known as Packer Meadow, named after a man who built a cabin in the meadow with the intention of homesteading. His plans were interrupted when the government granted a large portion of the land to the Northern Pacific Railroad. [Space, p. 21.]

From the time the expedition first crossed the Continental Divide at Lemhi, their food supply had been short. On a good day, they barely had enough to satisfy their appetites. They had tapped their emergency rations already, and the prospects of finding enough wild game to supply their needs was grim. Continuing down Packer Creek to the west end of the glade, they found a flat area where they spent the night.

September 14, 1805 – Up early, Whitehouse wrote, *"ate the last meat"*. Hunger was a gnawing, never ending, problem. A deer and a few birds did little to satisfy thirty-four people who were burning five thousand or more calories per day. The trek through the mountains was proving to be almost everything the captains had feared. Their struggles with nature were magnified with each mile and each day. The possibility of Captain Lewis' words, *". . . or purishes in the attempt"*, actually coming true haunted the Corps of Discovery. Nevertheless, they pushed ahead in a southerly direction. By passing the ridge trail (the Nez Perce road to the buffalo trail) to their right, they followed a well-beaten road over rough terrain through rain, hail, and snow. They were on the trail leading to the KoosKoosKee (Lochsa River). For fifteen miles, the horses and members of the party slipped and slid over downed timber. Their wet moccasins provided no traction as they dropped to the confluences of Crooked, Brushy and Colt

Killed Creeks. Crossing to the north side, they passed an area where the Indians (probably Nez Perce) had constructed two elaborate traps (weirs) for catching fish. All the grass had been eaten in this area, so they continued for two miles. Finding a place north of the river and opposite an island, they camped near the mouth of a stream. The island in the middle of the Lochsa River provided a good place for the horses. They swam them across to graze and left them overnight. This camp site is located south of U. S. Highway 12 at Powell Ranger Station. The island is now completely tree-covered. Having arrived, cold, wet, hungry and fatigued, they had nothing to eat but portable soup. Sergeant Gass wrote, "*. . . none of the hunters killed any thing except 2 or 3 pheasant; on which without a miracle it was impossible to feed 30 hungry men and upwards, besides some Indians.*" Captain Clark recorded, "*. . . here we compelled to kill a Colt for our men & Selves to eat for the want of meat & we named the South fork Colt Killed Creek.*"

Why The Lochsa?

Why did the party divert from the main and most direct trail westward? Was it planned or did Old Toby lead them astray? Were they hoping to find wild game or fresh salmon from the fall run? Captain Clark had explored the Salmon River as a possible navigable route to the Columbia. Were they exploring the possibility of floating the Lochsa to the Clearwater and then to the Columbia? Were they descending to get out of the snow? No one knows. None of the Expedition journalists seemed eager to blame Old Toby for this detour! For whatever reason, the trip down to the Lochsa cost them valuable time and energy.

September 15, 1805 – Off to an early start under cloudy skies, thirty-four people and a pack string of more than forty horses plodded along the north bank of the Lochsa. Over and around rocks, across streams and swampy areas, they followed the trail through dense underbrush for four miles. Private Whitehouse mentioned crossing a creek with a small pool just below it. Today, the creek is known as Wendover Creek and the pond, Whitehouse Pond. Both can be easily identified from U. S. Highway 12. Finding a two to three acre meadow, the party halted to let the horses graze and water. Old Toby recognized this area as a Salish fishery. "Just below the fishing place is a canon two or three miles long, impassible to horses." [C. V. Piper. Thwaites, *Original Journals of the Lewis and Clark Expedition*. Vol.

3, p.67, n. 2.] Assuming they had this information, there was but one choice: return to the ridge and resume travel along the Nez Perce Trail. Having time to barely catch their breath, the party began their ascent of approximately four thousand feet, out of the Lochsa canyon. The trail zigzagged with sharp turns up the south face of the mountain (Wendover Ridge). Downed timber was so thick they scarcely had a place to put their feet. Back and forth they climbed, single-file for hours. Their goal was to reach the Nez Perce Trail before dark. Horses, laden with heavy packs, toppled over and rolled down the steep incline. Captain Clark's writing desk was shattered as the horse carrying it lost its footing, rolling approximately one hundred and twenty feet before coming to rest against a tree. Luckily, the horse was able to stand once the packs were removed. Many people fell behind, completely exhausted. Two-thirds of the way up the mountain, Captain Clark found a spring where the leading party awaited the arrival of those lagging behind. Here, they collapsed, 'enjoyed' the view

Bald Spots

Captain Clark wrote, "maney parts bare of timber, they haveing burnt it down....as lies on the ground in every direction." From the beginning of the world as we know it, there have probably been bald areas in the Bitterroot Mountain Range similar to those seen today. Lightning caused forest fires and naturally occurring wind bursts produced large open areas throughout thickly timbered forest lands. Over time, the downed trees decayed, supplying a life supporting ecosystem for young seedlings. Green lush meadows grew where fires had raged. The scarred landscape was a beautiful mosaic supporting various forms of life specific to this geographic area. If not over grazed, the meadows seeded in, eventually and the nature cycle continued to repeat itself. To some extent, the combined practices of fire suppression, controlled burns and logging practices in the last century have taken the place of what nature once did. The U. S. Forest Service is presently re-evaluating its policies in light of several out of control burns within the last fifteen years which destroyed thousands of acres of timber. Most of the open or sparsely timbered areas which are seen today along the Lolo Trail are the result of naturally caused fires or clear cutting. The practices mentioned above have both drawbacks and benefits. The decisions are tough ones and, in reality, only time will tell if they were wise.

and had some portable soup to hold off the ever present threat of starvation. Captain Clark wrote, *"from this point I observed a range of high mountains Covered with snow from S.E. to S W with their tops bald or void of timber.* Both Sergeant Ordway and Private Whitehouse mentioned high rock clifts in this area. The rocks they were talking about are exposed granite and are a part of the Idaho Batholith. For two hours they waited. When all had arrived, they resumed their upward struggle to the summit to find there was no water. From a nearby, snow bank, they melted snow to drink. Dinner was two birds, a little left over colt and portable soup. The night was frigid. As they tried to sleep, the weather took a change for the worse. A moist weather system rolled up the western side of the mountains dumping its load of cold wet snow.

September, 16, 1805 – The Corps of Discovery awoke to three inches of snow, and by evening there was six to eight inches of new accumulation. They were miserable as they inched along the trail which often was completely obscured. Captain Clark, along with another member of the party, lead the way as they looked for trail signs, such as tree scars, bent or broken branches, resulting from the recent passage of travois or pack horses. As they found a sign, they would mark the trail clearly for the main party. Progress was slow. Heavy snow cascaded from laden limbs, obstructing their view. Everyone was cold and wet. Weary, exhausted, sleep deprived and starved, they must have wondered how they could continue. Private Whitehouse wrote, *"we mended up our mockasons. Some of the men without Socks raped rags on their feet.....".* Sergeant Ordway journaled, *"we mended our mockasons and Set out without anything to eat."* Finding no water, the party stopped at 1 p.m. to melt snow and drink their soup. Captain Clark's entry for the day was very descriptive. *"I have been wet and as cold in every part as I ever was in my life, indeed I was at one time fearfull my feet would freeze in the thin Mockirsons which I wore."* In spite of their discomfort, the trailblazers rushed ahead of the main party to locate a campsite, build a roaring fire and kill their second colt for dinner. Located in the vicinity of the Indian Post Office, this campsite is quite accessible today.

September 17, 1805 – The thaw was on and travel was miserable! For ten miles, ice cold water filled their moccasins as members of the Expedition sloshed down the deep grooves cut by feet and horse drawn travois. Would it ever end? Sacagawea and baby Pomp endured the same hardships. With a spirit rarely matched in history, they continued their forced march through the Bitterroot Range. Killing only two birds, they camped near a *"round deep Sinque hole full of water."* [Whitehouse] and killed their last colt.

Wolves (probably coyotes) howled through the night. Hearing these eery sounds, the hunters concluded they were near wild game.

September 18, 1805 – At the break of day, Captain Clark left with six hunters. Desperate for food, they were driven to reach the plains as soon as possible. There they hoped to find food and send it back to the main party. Before long, they reached a high mountain ridge sloping west (Sherman Peak). From here, Captain Clark spotted a large level plain to the west/southwest. Hope was renewed! After thirty-two gruesome miles, they camped on a large fast-moving creek with nothing to eat. The captain named the place Hungry Creek. Several miles back the main party struggled over rugged terrain until 3:00 p.m. with little water. Again they stopped to melt snow and drink a small amount of portable soup. They continued to follow the ridge separating the North Fork of the Clearwater and Lochsa Rivers in a southwesterly direction. After eighteen miles, they camped (Rocky Ridge). *"We dined & suped on a skant proportion of portable soupe, a few canesters of which, a little bears oil and about 20 lbs. Of candles form our stock of provision, the only recources being our guns and packhorses. The first is but a poor dependence in our present situation where there is nothing upon earth ex[c]ept ourselves and a few small pheasants, small grey Squirrels, and a blue bird of the vulter kind about the size of a turtle dove or jay bird."* – Captain Lewis.

September 19, 1805 – The advance party searched for game along Hungry Creek. Finding a stray horse, Captain Clark wrote, *"I derected him killed and hung up for the party after takeing a brackfast off for our Selves which we thought fine...."* Up and down mountains they went killing several birds including crows, ravens and a hawk. They camped on Cedar Creek not saying what they ate for dinner. Meanwhile, as Captain Lewis and the main party reached Sherman Peak, they were elated to see the wide-open flat land, too. Although it was approximately forty to sixty miles away, their faith was restored – they would not perish in these *"horrible mountains"* as Sergeant Gass called them. The excitement soon gave way to despair. They grew weaker and hungrier. Fear gripped them as they hugged steep rock walls on narrow ledges above deep canyons with their horses in tow. Captain Lewis recorded, *"Fraziers horse fell from the road . . . and roled with his load near a hundred yards into the Creek. We all expected that the horse was killed but to our astonishment . . . he rose to his feet & appeared to be but little injured . . . this was the most wonderfull escape I ever witnessed,"* Camping on the right side of a ravine, they sipped a small portion of their life-saving soup. Captain Lewis noticed several of his men had out breaks of sores and rashes, along with dysentery. Malnourished for almost a month, they must get some food and rest soon.

September 20, 1805 – Captain Clark and the hunting party found no game as they continued over rugged mountains. At twelve miles, they finally reached the west end of the Lolo Trail. Oh, the delight to be out of the mountains! They were on Weippe Prairie – home of the Nez Perce Indians. Back with the main party, horses were not hobbled as directed. The captain's horse with packs containing all his winter clothes and valuable Indian trade items was missing. Baptist Lepage, assigned to Captain Lewis' horse, was dispatched for the search, while others prepared to depart camp. Leaving at 10:00 a.m., they traveling a short distance before discovering the horse along with a note left by Captain Clark stating his intentions. Thrilled to have something to eat, they stopped for an early lunch. Meanwhile, Lepage returned empty-handed. Unwilling to give up the horse or merchandise, the captain dispatched two of the Corps' best woodsmen to continue the search, while the main party packed up the remainder of the "horse beef" and proceeded onto a ridge between Dollar and Sixbit Creeks. Camping there, Captain Lewis worked well into the evening describing several birds and plants until then unknown to science.

September 21, 1805 – While Captain Clark and his men were enjoying roots, berries and salmon with the friendly Nez Perce on Weippe Prairie, as usual, hungry wayward horses caused delay for the main party. Following in the advanced parties footsteps, they passed the September 19th Hungry Creek campsite of Captain Clark. Continuing on, they discovered a small meadow where they camped for the night (Camp Pheasant). Supper consisted of a few grouse, a prairie wolf (coyote), some crawfish and the remainder of their horse meat. Captain Lewis recorded, *"I find myself growing weak for the want of food and most of the men complain of a similar deficiency and have fallen off very much."* That night Captain Lewis determined he would order a forced march to the prairie the next day. Anticipating an early start, he directed the men to hobble all the horses. In spite of the order, one horse was missing, thus, detaining the party for some time. Eager to get out of the mountains, they ascended a ridge out of Lolo Creek to a small prairie, where they met Reuben Field with a supply of roots, berries and dried fish that Captain Clark purchased from the Nez Perce. Along with the food, Private Field brought good news. They were only seven miles from the Nez Perce village. After a one hour break, they walked through rough country arriving at the Indian camp around 5:00 p.m.. Sergeant Gass writes, *" arrived in a fine large meadow clear of these dismal and horrible mountains."* Though the Corps of Discovery rarely recorded expressions of emotion, Captain Lewis' excitement spills over in these words, *"the pleasure I now felt in having tryumphed over the rockey Mountains and decending once more to a level and fertile country where there was every rational hope of finding a comfortable subsistence for myself and party can be more readily conceived than expressed, nor was the flattering prospect of the final success of the expedition less pleasing."* The men sent to look for Captain Lewis' horse on September 20th, returned with the packs but no horse. As they were trying to catch up with the main party, they lost two horses, one of which was the captain's.

Captain Clark left five hunters on the Clearwater River when he returned to the village to greet the main party. With the exception of these men, the Corps of Discovery were together again for the first time in five days. Camping among the Nez Perce and along the Clearwater for approximately three weeks, the Corps of Discovery found an ample supply of food. However, they could hardly enjoy it. Severe stomach cramps and diarrhea kept most unwell for their entire stay. Attributing their discomfort to their initial gorging on roots and salmon when they first arrived, many returned to their old diet of venison. As they felt able, some members prepared dugout canoes for their trip down the Columbia to the ocean. Nez Perce chief, Twisted Hair, offered his assistance. He showed the weakened men how to burn the center of the logs and then hew out the charred insides. This process was much faster and easier than their previous methods. Others dug a hole to cache saddles and supplies unessential to their westward journey, branded horses to be left with the Nez Perce and gathered as much information as possible. The captains wanted to know

The Corps struggled mightily in the mountains of Idaho. Photo courtesy Jean Clary.

about water ways and other Indians they might encounter. The information provided by Chief Twisted Hair and other Nez Perce chiefs proved accurate.

October 7, 1805 – The Corps of Discovery set off on their voyage down the Clearwater, Snake and Columbia to the Pacific Ocean.

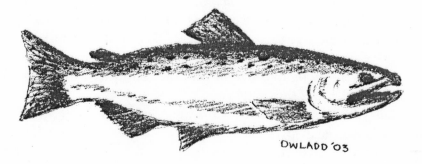

OWLADD '03

THE RETURN TRIP

June 10, 1806 – After a long wet winter at Fort Clatsop, on the coast (Oregon), the Corps of Discovery traversed up the steep, canyon wall of the Clearwater River then across Lolo (Collins) Creek canyon to the broad sweeping plains of Weippe Prairie. Having ascended approximately two thousand feet in a very short distance, they rose to a spectacular view. The camas were in full bloom giving the prairie the appearance of a lake of clear blue water. Seeing the snow covered mountains in front of them, they quickly realized their need for an Indian guide and extra horses. They felt they should have two horses for each member of the party – one to ride and one to pack. The captains set about making the necessary arrangements, while others procured a good supply of food and rounded up their horses. The Indians had tended the Corps' horses in addition to saving their supply cache from the rising Clearwater River, prior to their return from the Pacific coast. The Nez Perce would provide the needed guides but warned they should not attempt crossing the mountains for another month. Eager to return home, the captains ignored their advice and planned to set out right away. They waited for two days for the guides to return from a council meeting. Thinking they had waited long enough, impatience overrode good judgment. In hindsight, Captain Clark's premonition, *"Even now I Shudder with the expectation with great dificuelties in passing those Mountains"* should have been a red light, but everyone was ready to go! Captain Lewis wrote on the same night, *"convinced that we have not now any time to delay if the calculation is to reach the United States this season; this I am detirmined to accomplish if within the compass of human power.*"

The Corps of Discovery parted camp in a pouring rain on June 15, 1806, via the Lolo Trail. The wet ground gave way under the horses feet as they tripped over fallen trees. In no time, they were cold, wet and miserable. For two days, they muddled through the rain, passed old campsites and crossed familiar streams now raging from spring runoff. Soon, they were in snow five to ten feet deep and then eight to ten. With all the hardships the deep snow presented, there were some benefits: water was plentiful, barriers such as rocks and logs were covered with packed snow making travel for the horses less difficult. Only occasionally would the horses break through and sink to their bellies. Captain Lewis wrote, *"Here was winter with all it's rigors . . ."* However, they could not escape two glaring problems. Where was the trail? Where was forage for the horses? They must find both to get out of the mountains.

June 17, 1806 – Leaving their old Hungry Creek camp of September 10, 1805 and after several miles, they ascend a slope toward the hogback separating the Lochsa and North Fork of the Clearwater Rivers. Captain Clark took a small party to search for peeled trees and other signs marking the Nee Mee Poo Trail. Finding but a few spaced far apart, Droulliard, the Expedition's best frontiersman, no longer trusted his ability to find the trail. Captain Lewis would eat his words stated near Lemhi Pass in August of 1805, when he said, *"I felt perfectly satisfyed that if the Indians could pass these mountains with their women and Children, that we could also pass them."* "Retreat" was not a word a military expedition wanted to consider, so Captain Lewis decided to stop for two hours while he and Captain *Clark* conferred. In assessing their predicament, both concluded, *"we conceived it madnes in this stage of the expedition to proceed without a guide."* Indeed, the risks were too high. The decision was made they would cache everything they possibly could and retreat. A platform was constructed high above the snow on which journals, specimen, food and other nonessential items were stored and then covered with hides. The captains had made writing journals, sketching maps and collecting specimen a priority. For the first time since leaving St. Louis, these valuable items would not be in their personal care. Captain Lewis deemed them safer in the cache than with them. He feared the possibility that all or part might be washed away in the flood waters of Hungry Creek. After the cache was secured, the disheartened party returned to Hungry Creek where they camped for the night.

June 18, 1806 – At the crack of dawn, Droulliard and Shannon were dispatched to the Nez Perce camp in search of a guide. They were given permission to offer a gun to a trustworthy Indian willing to accompany the Corps of Discovery over the mountains to Travelers' Rest. If they had no takers, they could up the offer, if necessary, to three rifles and ten horses. As John Potts was clearing brush, he accidentally cut a large vein in his upper leg. Luckily, Captain Lewis knew where to apply pressure to stop the bleeding. The cut was apparently quite deep and needed stitches. Under less than ideal conditions, Captain Lewis cleaned, sutured and bandaged the wound. The excitement was not over. As they crossed the flood waters of Hungry Creek, John Colter's horse was swept downstream with him on it. Tumbling head over heels, through the boulder strewn torrent, the chances of their surviving looked slim. But, as often was the case with this expedition, the hand of providence brought both Colter and the horse through with little injury. Colter lost his blanket, but true to his frontier spirit, he emerged with gun in hand. By lunch they were at Fish Creek Meadow. Reuben and Joseph Field were left to hunt, while the main party proceeded to the confluence of Eldorado and Dollar creeks. They camped approximately one mile above their June 15th site.

June 19, 1806 – The captains planned to stay at this camp until guides arrived and they could resume their travel eastward. As the day warmed up, mosquitoes where out in force as some men fished. Finally, after catching nothing on gigs, Captain Lewis made a spear from a piece of metal he found in his pack. It worked well, but much to the men's disappointment, the fish were not chinook salmon but steel head trout for which they had yet to develop a taste.

June 20, 1806 – All hunters were dispatched in every direction to search for game. They returned with one poor cinnamon bear, seven steelhead and one deer, and little hope of finding more. Three horses and one mule were missing. Thinking they had probably gone back to the prairie for forage, the captains decided to return also in hopes of restocking their depleted food supply and to check on the welfare of Droulliard and Shannon.

June 21, 1806 – Parting camp for the prairie, the Corps left two horses with health problems behind. Much to their surprise, they met two young Nez Perce at Lolo Creek, along with their three horses and one mule lost the day before. Expecting to see Droulliard and Shannon with the young Indians, the captains became concerned when they discovered they were not with them. Communicating was very challenging, but after much effort, Captain Lewis gleaned enough information to determine the young Nez Perce were going across the mountains. The Captain persuaded them to stay until Droulliard and Shannon returned, after which they could accompany the Corps of Discovery. The young men agreed to wait at Crane Meadows for two days while the party returned to their old camp on the eastern edge of Weippe Prairie. Captain Lewis decided to leave Sergeant Gass and the Fields brothers at Camp Pheasant on Lolo Creek to hunt until the main party returned.

June 22, 1806 – A beautiful day west of the Rockies. The decision to return to the prairie proved fruitful. The hunters quickly killed eight deer and three bears. Spring chinook salmon were running in large numbers on the Clearwater. Captain Clark dispatched Whitehouse to the Clearwater with a good supply of trade beads to purchase some. In spite of everything positive, Captain Lewis had major concerns. John Pott's leg was infected. Where were Droulliard and Shannon? Would they get a guide? If not, would the young Indians at Crane Meadows grow restless and cross the mountains without them? The fears intensified. Captain Lewis treated Pott's leg by wrapping it in a poultice to reduce the inflamation.

June 23, 1806 – The captain sent Privates Frazier and Weiser to Crane Meadow to see if the young Indians were still there. If they were, the Corps men were to try and persuade them to wait a little longer. If they had gone, Sergeant Gass, the Fields brothers and Weiser were to *".... accompany the Indians by whatever rout they might take to travellers rest and blaize the trees well as they proceeded and wait at that place untill our arrivall with the party."*- Captain Lewis. The captain's fears had been justified. Frazier waited with his lame horse while the other followed the Indians. Meanwhile, Whitehouse, Droulliard and Shannon returned around mid-afternoon, having accomplished their missions. Three Nez Perce guides would accompany the Corps of Discovery across the mountains for the price of two rifles to be delivered on their arrival at Travelers' Rest. They were eager to start the journey, but there was one problem. John Colter had not returned from hunting. Ordering the horses hobbled for the night, the captains planned to get an early start the next morning.

June 24, 1806 – Colter arrived at the crack of dawn having killed a bear. The captains decided not to retrieve the bear but to saddle their horses and to be on their way. Accompanied by three Nez Perce guides, the party joined Frazier at Pheasant Camp, and then proceeded on to Eldorado Creek where they had earlier camped for several days. That evening, the Nez Perce guides set two huge fir trees on fire. The flames crowned the trees immediately. Captain Lewis wrote, *"They are a beatiful object in this situation at night. The exhibition reminded me of a display of fireworks."* The guides had flamed the trees to insure good weather for the mountain crossing.

June 25, 1806 – Battling mosquitoes and black flies, the guides lead the party over Mex Mountain to Fish Creek Meadows where they were reunited with the Fields brothers. They had killed nothing. Droulliard and Shields were dispatched to look for two horses that had strayed during the retreat. One of the guides was sick, and two others dropped back to be with him as the party proceeded through dense timber to Hungry Creek, where they found lush feed for the horses. After a short rest, they continued to a place north of Boundary Peak where they camped for the night, and by this time the sick guide and his two companions had arrived. Captain Lewis noticed one of the guides was very cold. He was dressed in his summer skins and thin moccasins-having brought no other clothing. Convinced the guides were committed to their word, the captain gave the sick guide one of his buffalo robes for which the young man was most grateful. Here, Sacagawea brought Captain Lewis a root (Jerusalem Artichoke) which he recognized as a Shoshone food.

June 26, 1806 – Leaving camp (Buffalo Robe) at 6:00 a.m., the party rode along the rugged canyons wall to their treetop cache. Finding the cache just as they had left it, they gathered the contents, packed them quickly and were on their way. While members of the Corps carried out their assigned duties, the captains took field notes. Captain Clark sketched geographical features, while Captain Lewis continued to describe plants and animals specific to the area. The snow pack had receded four feet since they were last here. The guides hurried them eastward in order to reach the next meadow before dark. Rain hampered their travel along the hogback as their horses slipped and slid over the treacherous snow pack. Reaching a lush meadow on the south side of Bald Mountain, they halted to give the horses time to graze. Realizing they would not make the next meadow 'til well after dark, they decided to remain there for the night. Every place void of deep snow was covered with large blooming plumes of bear grass. Although the horses never ate it, they managed to find ample forage between the large tufts. Late in the day, a Chopunnish from a village on the Clearwater joined the party. He told the captains he would accompany them to the great falls of the Missouri. While talking with him, Captain Lewis learned for the first time why the two young Indians were crossing the mountains. They were meeting some Flathead Indians near the mouth of Lolo Creek for a party. This camp site is located east of Sherman Peak and is near today's U.S. Forest Service lookout, Castle Butte. A Nez Perce guide told the party that when his people traveled with women and children, the men often dropped off the main trail to the fisheries on Colt Killed Creek, rejoining the Nez Perce band near the quamash glade.

June 27, 1806 – Breaking camp at 8:00 a.m., the party resumed travel following a beautiful scenic route along the high ridge separating the North Fork of the Clearwater and the Lochsa Rivers. Arriving at a rock cairn the Nez Perce called *"the smoking place"*, today's Indian Post Office, the guides requested they stop for a smoke. From this mountain top vista, the Corps of Discovery had a three hundred and sixty degree view of the Bitterroot Mountain Range. Their guides spoke of large herds of *white buffalo* in the mountains to the south. Captain Lewis wrote, ".... *from this place we had an extensive view of thes stupendous mountains principally covered with snow like that on which we stood; we were entirely surrounded by those mountains from which to one unacquainted with them it would have seemed impossible ever to have escaped; in short without the assistance of our guides I doubt much whether we who had once passed them could find our way to Travellers rest in their present situation for the marked trees on which we had placed considerable reliance are much fewer and more difficult to find than we had apprehended. These fellows are most admireable pilots.. . ."* After the short stop, they continued to Spring Mountain where they camped and dined on bear's oil and roots.

This photograph of Lolo Pass taken after the 1910 burn provides an excellent example of the deep snow that each winter brings to the area. Photo courtesy U.S. Forest Service.

June 28, 1806 – Needing food and water for the horses, the guides assured the party they would reach a good meadow by noon. Mounted on their horses high above the Lochsa River, the Corps of Discovery rode for six miles where they passed their old campsite (Snow Bank Camp) of September 15. Surely they remembered how miserably wet and cold they had been nine months ago. Continuing a little further, they noticed the trail to the right descending Wendover Ridge. This was the steep timber strewn path they had taken out of Lochsa canyon. Now, they were on a section of the Nee Mee Poo trail, they had never traveled. As promised by their guides, they arrived at the large open meadow by noon. The hungry horses were gaunt. They needed sufficient time to graze and rest. So after thirteen miles, the party halted for the afternoon and the night. (Thirteen Mile Camp).

June 29, 1806 – As usual, on the return trip, they mounted up and headed out early. They were not nearly as fatigued and hungry as they were going west – maybe saddle sore! Traveling for approximately five miles, they came to the ridge's end and made a steep descent into the Crooked Fork drainage. Crossing Crooked Creek, a major tributary of the Lochsa, they found a deer left by the hunters. Here, Captain Lewis bid "*adieu to the*

An old U.S. Forest Service sign near the Lolo Hot Springs provides insight into the use of the area by the Corps of Discovery.

snow." Ascending out of the canyon, they crossed the trail where on September 14, 1805, Old Toby, *reportly*, had misled the party down to the Lochsa. He had taken the Corps of Discovery on a terrible side trail when leaving the hot springs but apparently picked up the Nez Perce Trail again. The old trail led eastward, passing their Glade Creek campsite and then to Glade (Packer) Meadow. The camas were starting to bloom. They were flowering at least three weeks later than those seen at Weippe Prairie. Stopping just long enough for lunch, they continued along the trail crossing the divide from the Lochsa drainage (Idaho) to that of the Bitterroot (Montana). In no time, members of the Corps of Discovery along with their Indian guides were enjoying the warm waters of the hot springs. Staying in the warm water as long as they could stand it, the Indians would jump out quickly and emerge themselves in the ice cold water of Lolo Creek. Staying in the creek just long enough to cool down a bit, they quickly returned to the warm water. Back and forth they went. Captain Lewis tested the bath. He stayed in for nineteen minutes before having to get out. Spotting the footprints of two Indians, near the springs, the guides began to worry about their Ootlashoot friends. They feared they had been attacked and the prints were those of two Indians escaping the Minnetares. With enough food in this area and a large place to camp, they enjoyed this old Indian resort through the night.

June 30, 1806 – Having had success killing game, Droulliard and Joseph Field were sent ahead to hunt. As the main party prepared to leave the springs, a deer wandered in for water. The deer was shot and loaded on a packhorse. En route to Travelers' Rest, Captain Lewis' horse slipped on a steep hillside, throwing him off. Both tumbled for approximately forty feet before stopping. At one time, the captain came close to being pinned under his horse. Fortunately, neither were injured. Traveling thirteen miles, they stopped for lunch at their old campsite of September 12, 1805. The does were fawning so both whitetail and mule deer were abundant. From the mouth of Graves Creek to Travelers' Rest, the main party picked up three the hunters had shot and left for them. *"Descended the mountain to Travellers rest leaveing those tremendious mountanes behind us – in passing of which we have experiensed Cold and hunger of which I shall ever remember,"* Captain Clark wrote.

The "Living Witness Tree" at the Travelers' Rest site, a Douglas fir. Please see the sidebar about the Douglas fir on page 74. Photo courtesy Patricia Hastings.

Chapter 5

NOTES ON NATURE

At the conception of the exploration of the newly acquired territory west of the Mississippi River, President Thomas Jefferson laid into the hands of Lewis and Clark instructions that clearly reflected his passion, his thinking, and his persistent preoccupation with scientific matters. Since this responsibility carried with it the prestige of the President of the United States, Lewis and Clark regarded the instructions as a mandate and steadfastly recorded observations on temperature and rainfall, mountains and interlocking streams, animals, plants, and Indians of the land through which they passed, and committed their findings as entries in their journals.

Lewis contributed importantly to the development of American zoology by making the first faunal studies in the unexplored land by observing "the animals of the country generally, & especially those not known in the U. S." (Thwaites 7, p.249) Of the 122 species of animals recorded by Lewis and Clark, twelve were fish, fifteen were amphibians or reptiles, fifty were birds, and forty-five were mammals.

Additionally, Lewis greatly enriched American botany by making the first studies of plants indigenous to the western plains, mountains, deserts and river valleys; he collected and preserved specimens of herbs, shrubs and trees in these remote areas, extending the known range of many plants east of the Mississippi. The most important tangible botanical result of the Expedition was a collection of more than 200 dried, preserved specimens that comprise today the Lewis and Clark Herbarium in the Academy of Natural Sciences of Philadelphia.

Many of the animals and plants recorded in the journals were new to science. Overall, Lewis described them in language sufficiently detailed and technical as to make identification possible for later naturalists who read his descriptions.

Armed with his traveling library, Lewis could refer to books such as Professor Dr. Benjamin Smith Barton's *Elements of Botany* (the first textbook of botany written in the United States), a two volume edition of Linnaeus, and the four volumes called *"Owen's Dictionary"* – *A New and Complete Dictionary of Arts and Science.*

Telescoping our focus of interest to the Corps of Discovery's campsite located near the junction of Travelers' Rest Creek (Lolo Creek) and the Clark's or Flathead River (Bitterroot River) in September 1805 and again in June and July 1806, let us rediscover the species of flora and fauna seen and recorded in the journals. These entries give us a window into the variety of animals, birds, plants and trees encountered at Travelers' Rest and vicinity.

FLORA

Trees

Situated on the crest of a small hill south of the Corp's latrine stands an aged sentinel. It is a Douglas fir tree measuring four feet in diameter and ninety-five feet tall. Because it has watched centuries of activities occurring just beyond the shade of its branches, it has earned the title of a "Living Witness Tree". During its lifetime, the fir has been witness to human life at this trail-crossing and stopping spot, and much later viewed settlers working the nearby landscape.

As Lewis neared the campsite of September 9th, he observed, *"pine principally of the long leafed kind with some spruce and a kind of furr resembling the scotch furr".* (Thwaites 3, p.57) In Lewis' terminology regarding softwoods (conifers), the "Long leaf pine" is the Ponderosa pine, *Pinus ponderosa,* that later, in 1949, became the Montana state tree; "Spruce pine" is the Engelmann spruce, *Picea engelmannie,* *"fur resembling the scotch furr"* is the Douglas fir, *Pseudotsuga menziesii,* and the "Short leaf pine" noted on September 12th is the Lodgepole pine, *Pinus contorta.* While crossing mountain peaks on September 14th, the "fur" trees Clark saw were the Subalpine fir, *Abies lasiocarpa,* and the *"Tamearack",* the Western larch, *Larix occidentalis.* (See drawings on opposite page.)

If it seems there was a special interest in "needled" trees upon arriving in the Bitterroots, focus was on the leaved (deciduous or hardwood) trees on

Some of the conifers noted in the journals

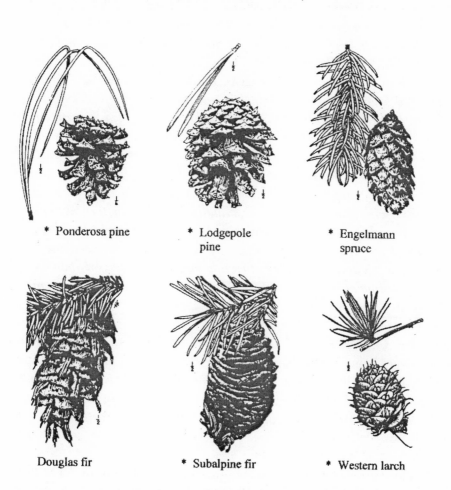

* Ponderosa pine   * Lodgepole   * Engelmann
                       pine   spruce

Douglas fir   * Subalpine fir   * Western larch

Scale of reduction from specimen size is indicated by fractions.
*= trees previously unknown to science

(Little, p. 39-44)

the return. On July 2, 1806, Lewis described the "leaf of the cottonwood on this river" being wider than that of the cottonwoods on the upper part of the Missouri River; this is the Black cottonwood, *Populus trichocarpa*. Another hardwood was the "alder aspin" – the Quaking aspen, *Populus tremuloides*. The River birch, *Betula occidentalis*, grew in the riparian area.

Shrubs

Chokecherries, *Prunus virginiana*, grew in abundance around Travelers' Rest and impressed Sergeant Whitehouse, as he wrote on September 10th, "*the choke cherries abound on its bottoms. The natives has lately gathered an amence quantities of them here for food.*" (Thwaites 7, p.153) Other shrubs such as the "narrow leafed willow – the Sandbar willow, *Salix exigua*, "broad leaf willow" – possibly the Bebb willow, *Salix bebbiana*, the "elder" – Common elderberry, *Sambucus Canadensis*, and Serviceberry, *Amelanchier alnifolia*, also grew in the area.

During the Bitterroot Mountain transit those shrubs new to science included an alder with reddish-brown bark and common to elevations over four thousand feet – the Sitka alder, *Alnus sinuate*, a *"redwood honeysuckle"*, probably the shrub known as Red Twinberry or Utah honeysuckle, *Lonicera utahenesis* (Moutlon 13, p.171), and the low growing bush *"common to the hights of the mountains"* that Lewis described as *"whortleberry"*, the Western huckleberry, *Vaccinum membranaceum*.

Herbaceous Plants

On the return trek, after the party passed the Glade Creek encampment of September 13, 1805, they arrived at the "quawmas flats" by noon and stopped to dine and graze the horses. Lewis described this area, today called Packer Meadows, as *"a pretty little plain stocked with quawmash"*, a plant known as camas. Seventeen days prior, Lewis had reached the two thousand level acres of the Weippe Prairie where the camas were in full bloom. He exclaimed, the camas *"resembles lakes of fine clear water, so complete is this deseption that on first fight I could have sqoarn it was water"*. *(Thwaites 5, p.132)*

A member of the Lily family, Camas, *Camassia quamash*, was one of the new to science plants Lewis collected and brought back to Philadelphia.

The flowering stems of this perennial are eight to twenty inches tall and arise from a brownish-coated egg-shaped bulb. The narrow grass-like leaves also grow upward from near the base. The three petals and three sepals are so similar in appearance, there looks to be six petals. These are spread widely to form light blue star-shaped flowers. The plants have short individual flower stalks blooming a few at a time from the bottom upward. The six stamens have yellow anthers. Camas commonly grows in meadows that are wet during the spring and dry in late summer, and from valleys to the lower subalpine zone. They bloom from May to July, depending on elevation and snow cover.

Lewis described the bulb-shaped root to be the size of a nutmeg or as large as a hen's egg. Camas bulbs were an important food source for the Salish and Nez Perce Indians.

A day before arriving at Travelers' Rest, one small member of the cactus family made an acute impression on the party. Clark wrote in his journal, *"on this part . .[of].. .Clarks River I observed great quantities of a peculiar Sort of Prickly peare grow in Clusters ovel & about the Size of a Pigions egge with Strong Thorns which is So birded as to draw the Pear from the Cluster after penetrating our feet."* *(Thwaites 3, p.56-57)* This was the Brittle prickly pear, *Opuntia fragilis,* a plant new to science. Another name for it is Jump cactus, a mat-forming plant that is found on dry grassland slopes in the foothills of the Sapphire Range.

Lewis preserved at least four previously undescribed plant species while at Travelers' Rest; the Small-head (or wooly) clover, *Trifolium microcephalum*, *"with a very narrow small leaf and a pale red flower"*, the Wormleaf stonecrop, *Sedum stenopetalum*, the Thinleaf owlclover, *Orthocarpus tenuifolius*, and the Bitterroot, *Lewisia rediviva*, a plant he had

---

The Camas Oven

As food gatherers, the Nez Perce women were responsible for digging the camas roots, or gémes, from June through September, depending on site elevations. Their digging stick, a tùk'es, a two and a half foot long wooden staff with a fire-hardened point bent slightly upwards. The five to eight inch crosspiece handle was made of bone, horn or wood. To operate the stick, both hands were placed on the handle and body weight was applied until the point reached a depth of about six inches in the ground. Cylindrical carrying baskets were used to transport the roots to camp where, prior to baking, the women and children cleaned off the dark outer coating. The roots were never eaten raw.

To prepare the baking oven, a circular pit was dug in the ground, measuring two and a half feet deep and ten feet in diameter. Dried kindling was put in the bottom; next, large stones were placed onto the wood that was then set on fire to heat the stones until they became red-hot. Then earth was sprinkled over them, topped with alder leaves and then a layer of meadow grass. The camas roots were placed upon these layers, and another layer of leaves and more meadow grass were added to cover the bulbs. Next, water was thrown on top of this pile; steam was created when the moisture reached the hot rocks below. Lastly, a four-inch layer of earth was added to cover the mound and a fire was built on top. It continued to burn ten to twelve hours, after which it cooled for two to three days.

Upon removal from the baking oven, the roots are as sweet as molasses. For immediate consumption the cooked roots can be made into porridge. As baked camas does not store well, it was usually pounded and dried as a meal called kom'es'es *and formed into loaves, rolled in bunch grass and again steamed. After cooking, the loaves were made into smaller cakes known as* ep'me *and dried in the sun or over a campfire and stored for winter use, complementing dried fish. (James p.12-14)*

At Travelers' Rest, Lewis
preserved these four previously
undescribed plant species

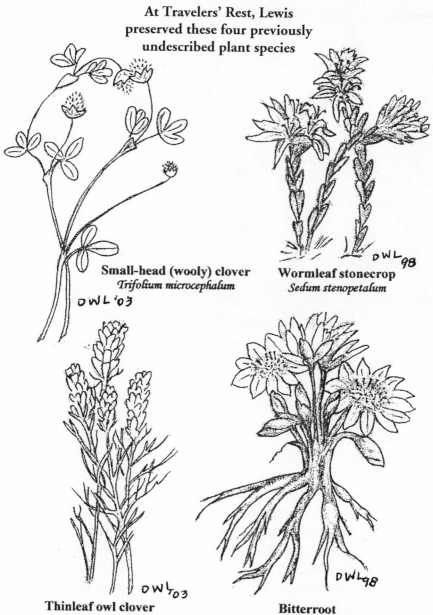

Small-head (wooly) clover
Trifolium microcephalum

Wormleaf stonecrop
Sedum stenopetalum

Thinleaf owl clover
Orthocarpus tenufolius

Bitterroot
Lewisia rediviva

Beargrass in bloom.
Photo courtesy Patricia Hastings.

initially described on August 22, 1805, and had found the root bitter to the taste, although the Shoshone Indians would eat them heartily. The Bitterroot plant, named after Meriwether Lewis, blooms in late May and June. The succulent leaves are visible for several months before withering, when the dark buds then appear and produce pale pink or even white to deep rose blossoms. The flower, measuring one and a half to three inches across, consists of about fifteen rounded or pointed overlapping petals. These plants prefer dry prairies to foothill ridges of rocky or shallow soil. It has long been a tradition of the Natives of Western Montana to annually dig for these roots; it was an event of great sociability and much significance. In the Bitterroot Valley, other Salisan tribes joined the resident Flathead Indians during May, the "Bitterroot month". The plants' roots were valued for their starch content. The Bitterroot Valley, Bitterroot River and the Bitterroot Mountains are named after this plant, which became Montana's State Flower in 1895.

Near Bald Mountain on the return journey, Lewis remarked on *"a great abundance of Species of bear grass which grows on every part of those Mountains, its growth is luxuient and continues green all winter but the horses will not eat it."* *(Thwaites 5, p.162)* Earlier while at the Weippe Prairie he had noted

Brittle prickly pear cactus. Photo courtesy Patricia Hastings.

that this grass was used by the Natives to make baskets and other ornaments. Beargrass, *Xerophyllum tenax*, produces stalked white flowers borne in a terminal inflorescence that is at first cylindrical but becomes greatly elongated as the flower matures. Beargrass is common on open slopes in subalpine zones. This was a species new to science.

On the day of arrival, June 30th, Lewis showed Clark a trailside *"plant in blume which is sometimes called the lady's slipper or mockerson flower"*, the Mountain lady's slipper, *Cypripedium montanum*, a rare species unknown to science.

For further reading and for a nature tour of the Lolo Trail, an excellent resource is Sharon Ritter's book, *Mountain Wilds*.

FAUNA

Birds

On the outbound journey through the Bitterroot Valley, focus was upon securing food to satisfy hunger and the preparation to cross the snowy mountains to the west. As game birds were shot for the dinner pot, usually little attention was made to species' descriptions; but with a few clues we can put the puzzles together. We read of killing *"pheasents, crains, prarie fowl, wild geese, ducks and grouse".* The pheasant *"of the Common kind"* having a black tail and a red stripe above the eye is a Spruce (or Franklin's) grouse. The large, dark colored species with some white feathers scattered on the neck, breast and belly is the Blue (or Richardson's) grouse; and the *"prarie hen"* or fowl with the short pointed tail is the Sharp-tailed grouse. The cranes are Sandhills, and the wild geese, most likely, the Canada geese; the ducks could be a large variety of species. Lewis examined one bird brought in by his hunters that was a *"redheaded woodpecker of the large kind common to the U. States" (Thwaites 3, p.57)* – the Pileated woodpecker, and later referred to as the "logcock".

The Franklin or spruce grouse.
Illustration courtesy Diann Ladd.

Trekking the Lolo Trail, Crows and Ravens were seen; Lewis also described three birds new to science: the Varied thrush, and *"two birds of a blue colour both . . . of the haulk or vulture kind".* One had a blue sheen appearance with a high tuft of feathers on the head – the Steller's jay, and the other, with a white head and made notes resembling the mewing of a cat – the Gray jay.

During the 1806 return passage and enforced stay at Camp Chopunnish on the Clearwater River, Lewis made a number of important bird observations and discoveries. He gave a clear and unmistakable description of the beautiful Western tanager, declaring *"the plumage is remarkably delicate; that of the neck and head is of a fine orange yellow and red . . . the tail, back and wings are black". (Thwaites 5, p.111)* He gave closer examination to a bird he previously thought to be a species of woodpecker that was Robin sized, fed on the seeds of pine trees, had a white tail, black wings and a light brown body. However, this was a bird in the family of crows and jays and later was to be named the Clark's nutcracker, after William Clark. Another bird Lewis termed the *"black woodpecker"* was ultimately named after him, the Lewis' woodpecker, a bird with a crimson red throat, the belly and breast a mixture of red and white, wings and head black with a glossy tint of green. In 1806 Lewis brought back specimens of these three birds, previously unknown to science. Upon his request of Alexander Wilson, a bird illustrator, Wilson not only drew from these very specimens, but also named them. One he called the Louisiana (now Western) tanager, another the Lewis's woodpecker, and the third, Clark's crow (now Clark's nutcracker). In 1811 these drawings appeared together on Plate XX in Volume III of Wilson's nine-volume work, *American Ornithology*. (See page 99 for color photo.)

Upon returning to Travelers' Rest in 1806, Lewis listed the birds *"found in this vally"* as the *"dove [Mourning dove], the black woodpecker [Lewis' woodpecker], the lark woodpecker [Northern flicker], the log cock [Pileated woodpecker], the prarie lark [probably the Western meadowlark: (In 1931 this became the Montana State bird)], sandhill crain [Sandhill crane], prarie hen with the short and pointed tail [Sharp-tailed grouse], the robin [American robin], a species of brown plover [?], a few curloos [Long-billed curlew], small black birds [likely the Brewer's blackbird], ravens, hawks, and a variety of sparrows as well as the bee martin [Western kingbird] and several species of Corvus genus [Crows, Jays and Ravens]." (Thwaites 5. p.176-177)*

All the birds the Expedition observed in the Bitterroot Valley and in crossing the mountains to the west are still to be seen in these areas today. However, there was yet one species Lewis was soon to encounter that we will not find. On July 5, 1806, as Lewis' band was moving north from present-day Bonner, Montana, he reported, *"a great number of pigeons breeding in this part of the mountains." (Thwaites 6, p.221)* A year prior, on August 26th, Clark noted having seen *"Some fiew Pigions"* near the mouth of the Lemhi River. These were the only recorded sightings of the Passenger pigeon, *Ectopistes migratorius*, west of the Continental Divide.

We can be confident that there was no mistake in the identification, because the Captains were well acquainted with these pigeons and would not have confused them with others of similar appearance, such as the Mourning dove, which Lewis identified on July 1st at Travelers' Rest. There was a substantial size difference between pigeons and doves; the passenger pigeon was sixteen inches long, and the mourning dove is twelve inches. The dove also has a white eye ring and a small dark spot on the side of the face.

Passenger pigeons were once the most abundant bird in the world. John. J. Audubon, Alexander Wilson, and other early ornithologists give accounts about this pigeon which seem beyond imagination. Audubon describes flocks that he calculated at more than a billion birds passing en masse for three days. "The light of the noon day was obscured as if by eclipse . . . The dung fell . . . not unlike melting flakes of snow." (Griggs) The flocks lived on the nuts and fruits of the original eastern American forest. Following food sources, they wandered indiscriminately and nested in dense colonies up to forty miles long and several miles wide. Their numbers made commercial harvesting by gunners, netters, and dynamiters profitable. "Wagon loads of them are poured into market . . . and Pigeons become the order of the day at dinner, breakfast and supper, until the very name becomes sickening", Wilson reported in 1814.

Passenger pigeons and the eastern forest were destroyed simultaneously. By the end of the 19th century little was left of either. The last major pigeon nesting occurred near the shore of Lake Michigan in 1881 and in Wisconsin in 1882, but this bird could not sustain itself in small to moderate numbers. The last one, "Martha," died at the Cincinnati Zoo in 1914.

Early in the Expedition Lewis wrote of the many pigeons passing overhead in migration, and in September 1804 he commented on the animals and pigeons that were feeding on a new crop of acorns.

We are fortunate to have the journal notes regarding this bird, and to learn the extent of the western range of this species that has since bowed to extinction.

As a note of interest, on the Expedition's return, as Captain Lewis approached the junction of the Marias and Missouri Rivers in July 1806, he still had a little bread of cows (bricks of dried Cous root) remaining of which he and his men made a kettle of mush together with a few pigeons they had killed. The following day he and Reuben Field killed nine pigeons roosting in the trees near camp; on these they dined.

Insects

Stand anywhere near water along the Lolo Trail in July and you have only to wait a few seconds before being bitten and having offered blood, blood given the same way as that of the members of the Expedition. The messengers responsible for this blood sacrifice are the species of mosquitoes, *Aedes vexans.* The females do the biting, as they require a special supplement of protein from an animal in order to mature their eggs. Imagine, mosquitoes that suck blood from your exposed skin could be direct descendants of those who bit the men of the Expedition!

Lewis once claimed that mosquitoes were one of "our trio of pests" – prickly pear and gnats were the other two. A thriving infestation of mosquitoes haunted the campsite of Travelers' Rest. Patrick Gass thought they were worse here than any place he had known since the party had left the Old Maha village, near present-day Homer, Nebraska. These insects tormented Clark to the degree that he could not write in his journal except while in the protection of his mosquito netting.

After the Captains separated on July 3, 1806, Lewis's first campsite was situated in a clearing near the junction of today's Clark Fork River and Grant Creek. Here, too the greeting committee consisted of a multitude of mosquitoes that even afflicted the horses. For the animals' relief, *"we were obliged to kindle large fires for our horses these insects torture them in such manner until they placed themselves in the smoke of the fires that I realy thought they would become frantic. About an hour after dark the air become so coald that the mosquetoes disappeared."* (Thwaites 5, p.183)

Columbian Ground Squirrel

On Clark's return through the Bitterroot Valley, he observed on July 3rd *"the burrowing Squirrel of the Species common about the quawmarsh flats West of the Rocky Mountains"* (Thwaites 5, p.246) While camping on the Weippe Prairie Lewis had killed several and found them tender and well flavored. The Columbian ground squirrel, *Citellus columbianus,* is one of the largest squirrels, commonly known by many as a "gopher." It has white spots on its gray back, and buff-colored sides that fade into the tawny under parts. This squirrel is fifteen inches long, including the three to four inch tail, weighs one and three-quarters pounds and hibernates during the winter. Enemies are hawks, eagles and meat eating animals. It is not gregarious and prefers its own burrow. However, it lives in large colonies that may extend for miles. Colonization helps in the survival of them all, for some members of the group are always on alert for danger while the rest are feeding. At the slightest speck in the sky, the air raid system of shrill whistles echo, as the alarm is passed on. When danger is passed, an all-clear chirp is given and activity is resumed. From a nest in their burrow, they raise one to twelve young each year.

Normally found in the mountainous sections of the Northwest, this squirrel feeds on wild vegetation. But when it moves onto the farms and ranch land it can be a nuisance, for the squirrels consume much of the forage and grain meant for livestock. In consuming this good food the "gophers" grow larger and also produce larger litters. The gophers then, become a problem to ranchers and are fair game for the marksman.

Red Squirrel

The Red squirrel, *Tamiasciurus hudsonicus*, is that noisy commentator of the forest activities. When undisturbed he produces a high-pitched chirp often mistaken for that of a bird. But when he's excited, his scolding, whistles and shrieks are accompanied with jerks and twitches of his upright tail. This energetic inhabitant of evergreen forests is fourteen inches long including a six-inch tail, weighs seven to nine ounces and does not hibernate. He eats the seeds of evergreens, acorns, mushrooms and the nuts of hickory, beech and walnut trees. His enemies are hawks, owls, snakes, foxes, bobcats, lynxes, martins and fishers.

Lewis described this small squirrel as one with a white belly that inhabits the timbered areas of the Rocky Mountains.

Summer and fall are intense periods of food gathering for the Red squirrel. Scampering up the tree he cuts off the cones with his teeth, dropping them to the ground. When spruce and subalpine fir cones are taken, green and sticky with gum, his coat can be matted with the gooey substance. He often has several preferred spots where he likes to sit while eating, discarding the unwanted parts on the ground forming heaps up to four feet in diameter and as many feet high. The Red squirrel is considered a tree squirrel because he prefers to occupy a hollow tree or empty woodpecker hole where he builds a leaf nest and raises the three to five young ones, born in April or May.

White-tailed and Mule Deer

"Deer are very abundant in the neighborhood of Travelers Rest of both species, also some bighorns and elk." (Thwaites 5, p.173) Lewis made his observation on June 30, 1806. During this three-day respite approximately twenty-one deer would be killed for food. These two species are the white-tailed deer, *Odocoileus virginianus,* and the mule deer, *Odocoileus hemionus.* Both Lewis and Clark were very familiar with the white-tailed deer in

Virginia and in the Ohio valley and referred to it as the "common deer of our country". From the very start of the journey, this species was frequently encountered; the hunters killed their first deer on May 19, 1804, just above St. Charles, Missouri.

Today the white-tailed deer is the number one game animal; it gets its name from the white underside of its twelve-inch tail that is displayed like a flag when the deer is alarmed or dashes off. A full grown buck stands thirty-four to forty inches high at the shoulder, measures four to five feet in length, and weighs over two hundred pounds. The doe is somewhat smaller.

The white-tail is the most widely distributed and most numerous species of deer in North America, ranging from southern Canada throughout the eastern United States stretching westward cross the Great Plains into the Rocky Mountains and south into Mexico. It is one of the few animals that has profited by man's activity. Its numbers have increased with the reduction of its natural predators, the clearing of deep forests improving its habitat, better hunting laws, and their rapid reproduction rate. In 1967 the national white-tail herd was estimated to exceed five million animals. This is an animal of open, well-watered woodlands, not of the deep forest, and its food consists of leaves, twigs and brush whose growth man stimulated when virgin forests were cut down.

On September, 17, 1804, in the vicinity of present-day Chamberlain, South Dakota, Clark described a new kind of deer killed by Private John Colter. It was ". . . *a curious kind of Deer of a Dark gray colour — or more so than common, hair long & fine, the ears large & long, a Small recepticle under the eyes like the Elk, the taile about the length of the Common deer, round [like a cow] a tuft of black hair about the end, this Species of Deer jumps like a goat or Sheep.*" *(Thwaites 1, p.152)* This deer was noted from then on, as far as the western slopes of the Rocky Mountains. Lewis was the first white man to record the deer at great length and coined its name, when in his journal entry of May 10, 1805, he wrote, *"There are several essential differences between the Mule deer and the common deer as well in form as in habits. . ."* *(Thwaites 2, p.20)* following which was an extended description of the body type and behavior.

The mule deer is a relative newcomer to the North American scene, a descendant of the white-tailed deer. The white-tail deer is the oldest of all the deer species in the western hemisphere, its first fossil records appearing some four million years ago, and appear to be identical to today's species of deer. After the North American glacial age, the white-tail inhabited the eastern areas, and its close relative, the black-tailed deer along the west coast.

As their ranges expanded, the white-tail west and north, and the black-tail eastward, they met. Their union created the western mule deer. Recently, researchers who used new investigative tools for determining heredity codes, discovered that the meeting of black-tails and white-tails provided the genetic origin of mule deer. The research was based on studies of DNA of the three kinds of deer. (Geist, p.27) In studying their mitochondrial DNA they discovered that all mule deer are descendants of white-tail deer does and black-tail deer bucks. (Geist, p.3)

The mule deer is stockier and more heavy-set than the white-tail, standing forty-two inches high at the shoulder and is six feet in length; does are smaller. The large ears resemble those of a mule and the tail features a black tip.

White-tails and mule deer display entirely different behavioral patterns. For instance, when white-tails run fast, they gallop and flag their white tails. Mule deer do not raise their black-tipped tails while fleeing. The "jumping" of the mule deer that Clark refers to in his journal, is the stiff-legged bounding gait when all four feet are off the ground at once. This movement is called "stotting". Apparently it allows the deer to escape predators that they might not otherwise be able to outrun, and enables them to jump over obstacles that a pursuing animal must go around. Actually, stotting is very costly in energy; bodily lift requires about thirteen times the energy spent in equal horizontal movement like galloping. Nevertheless, the stotting mule deer can suddenly depart at right angles to his line of travel, and even jump backward. Another difference between these two deer is their antlers; in white-tails the tines raise straight up from the main beam, while mule deer antlers are larger and "complex" averaging two sets of "Y"s and a single point on each beam.

During the winter stay at Fort Clatsop, Lewis recorded that the Columbian Black-tailed deer of that region was like that of the mule deer in that it bounded with all four feet off the ground at the same time, not loping as the common deer.

In Valerius Geist's book, *Mule Deer Country* he expresses his opinion that the mule deer is a species marked for extinction. For a number of reasons it has already lost much of its former range that ultimately was replaced with white-tail deer. Reading Geist's book is highly suggested for further study on this subject.

Grizzly Bears

Within journal excerpts, one can read that bighorn sheep and elk were

Listed as a "white buffalo" in the journals, the mountain goat frequented the mountains near Travelers' Rest. Photo courtesy Patricia Hastings.

also seen in the areas adjacent to Travelers' Rest, and the Corps' Indian guides had told them of the white buffalo (mountain goats) living in the high mountains to the south. On two days only were bears recorded in the Bitterroot area by any of the men. On the outbound route Ordway wrote on Sept. 12th, *"one of the hunters chased a bear up the Mountain but could not kill it." (Moulton 9, p.225)* Ten months later on July 3rd as Clark rode south in the Bitterroot Valley, he mentioned seeing a bear. We presume both were black bear sightings since neither author specified. The explorers saw no other live bears, black or grizzly. However, on September 11, 1805, they did remark upon a white bear (grizzly) skin hanging on a pine tree on which the Natives had painted figures. This was assumed to be *"a place of worship among them."*

The Indians believed in the immortality of all life; different spirits could come out of once living animals. Thus, a person could invoke mystic forces or spirits to be specially his own that would act as guide or protector. This relationship was called "Wyakin", which was one's faith in some strength to help in time of danger. One's Wyakin was initially revealed as a voice or apparition. Among the many apparitions that might be seen, the grizzly bear or buffalo bull meant strength in battle. (McWhorter, 1940, p. 296-8)

It seems surprising that the party did not encounter more bears in the vicinity of Travelers' Rest, because both species are indigenous to the Bitterroot Range of the Rocky Mountains. The Grizzly bear, *Ursus arctos horribilis*, has long been an object of a certain fascination, because it is the largest and most feared of the North American predators. Scientists believe it evolved in Siberia and passed from Asia into North America across the Bering Land Bridge during the last ice age. Spreading south it eventually occupied a swath of territory from Alaska to central Mexico and from California to Minnesota. Although a few early explorers had seen the Grizzly, notably Alexander Mackenzie, Lewis and Clark were the first to contribute factual data concerning its range, habits and physical characteristics. The Expedition encountered this species frequently on the Upper Missouri River and found them particularly troublesome in the vicinity of the Great Falls.

On the Expedition's return route, they camped for nearly a month by the Clearwater River near present-day Kamiah, Idaho, a site they called Camp Chopunnish or Long Camp. While there, Lewis gave great attention to the bears, not only in description but as a source of food. Besides providing a hearty meal, the oil or grease was saved as emergency trail food.

The bighorn sheep. Photo courtesy Patricia Hastings.

Ordway noted that five gallons of bear oil were put into kegs. The Nez Perce informed them that they called the grizzly "Hoh-host" and the black bear "Yâck-Kâh".

The grizzly, because of its ferocity and also by the variety of colors among the bears, intrigued Lewis; this led him to wonder if he was dealing with several species. On May 15th, he commented *"if we were to attempt to distinguish them by their collours and to denominate each colour a distinct species we should soon find at least twenty"*, (Thwaites 5, p38), and it would not be inappropriate to call them the "verigated" bear.

As noted, the grizzly has long roamed the area of the Bitterroot Mountains. After hibernating in the high country, the bears would go down the west slopes in the spring to feed on salmon or steelhead in several forks of the Clearwater River. Late April or early May they returned to higher ridges and mountainsides to eat tuberous plants and berries. By August they were back to the rivers to feed on the Chinooks (Dog Salmon), return once more to the hills for grubs, ants and berries, and then go higher to the alpine country to feed on ground squirrels and marmots. When the winter storms began, they denned up for the winter months, November to April.

It was inevitable that early settlers and grizzlies would clash in populated areas on the periphery of the Bitterroots. Bitterroot Valley homesteaders had plenty of problems with this bear. To obtain safe areas for farming and ranching, the pioneers waged an aggressive war of eradication against them. Trapping was the primary method; one valley trapper's cabin was located in the Big Sand Lake area just west of Blodgett Pass near Hamilton, Montana. In 1908 he killed five black bears and four grizzlies – perhaps even more. It is a conservative estimate that trappers operating around the turn of the century killed probably twenty-five to forty grizzlies in the Bitterroot Mountains each year.

Bear losses due to trapping and hunting were multiplied by the grazing of thousands of sheep after the 1910 wild fires denuded the forests. Homesteaders from both sides of the Bitterroot Mountains grazed cattle on mountain meadows in areas inhabited by grizzlies. Stockmen feared bears, especially the grizzly, and killed every one they saw near their bands. Up to the mid 1930s, one area of sheep grazing was at Packer Meadows on Lolo Pass where bear confrontation was always a concern. (Moore, Ch 17)

The remaining grizzly bears sustained further hardship when, in 1927, the Inland Power and Light Company erected a dam across the Clearwater River at Lewiston, Idaho. Fish ladders were furnished but were ineffective, reducing the run of red salmon and eliminating the dog salmon from the entire Clearwater River drainage. This finally caused the demise of a once abundant population of grizzlies. By the mid 1940s the bears that had once flourished in the Bitterroot Mountains lost the battle for survival.

Long ago there was an Indian prophet named Swopscha, who predicted the coming of a strange white-skinned people who would come to the Clearwater and adjacent Nez Perce country. Some of the things these strangers would bring with them would be new and wonderful; others would be harmful and dangerous. At first they would be friendly, but wars and bloodshed would follow. Sickness and diseases would wipe out entire tribes. All creation would be overthrown, the buffalo exterminated, elk and deer fenced in, Indians confined, game disappearing and rivers held back, no longer providing Salmon to the tribes. These Nez Perce prophecies were passed from one generation to another in "Dream Songs". (McWhorter, 1952, p. 77)

In 1982 the Grizzly bear won the honor to become the animal symbol for the State of Montana.

Domestic sheep grazing on Packer Meadow in the 1930's. Photo Courtesy Bud Moore.

Chapter 6

THE NEZ PERCÉ

From their first day at Travelers' Rest in 1805 to their final departure from this welcome stop on both their outbound and return journeys, the Nez Perce Indians were to play a significant role with the Corps of Discovery's efforts.

While knowing, in early September of 1805, that they would ultimately come into the land of the Nez Perce on their journey over the Bitterroot Mountains to the west of Travelers' Rest, their first encounter with the Nez Perce occurred in the vicinity of Travelers' Rest – and it was unexpected if eventful. John Colter, one of the hunters in the field for the day while the party was encamped at Travelers' Rest, stumbled upon three young Nez Perce warriors, and after establishing peace among themselves, the young Indians came back to camp with Colter, even though they were in hot pursuit of some Shoshone who had audaciously run off with twenty-one Nez Percé horses.

After a meal with the Explorers, one of the young Indian men decided he would go back over the Bitterroot Mountains with the Expedition to acquaint them with his people. That did not work out, and perhaps it was very unfortunate. There is speculation today that Old Toby and his son, the Expedition's Shoshone guides, would probably have been more familiar with the southern and, or middle route over the mountains than the northern Lolo Trail. Maybe the young Nez Percé could have gotten the Corps of Discovery over the Bitterroots easier and sooner. He would have been more familiar with the northern route – the old Indian Trail to the Buffalo that his people had used for generations.

Stray horses and impatience, however, led the young Nez Perce to take off and follow his friends. However, the young men had given the explorers two valuable pieces of geographical information about the land ahead of them: first, from his people's land over the mountains there was a good, navigable waterway to the ocean; and second, there was an easy pass to the east of Travelers' Rest, over the divide to buffalo country, accessible by, or following, water (today's Clark Fork), which could be picked up a few miles north of Travelers' Rest (their present camp), and then a few miles east meet with another river (today's Blackfoot River).

This confirmed what Old Toby had told them the day before, and they made a note to check that out on the return spring trip. The "too good to be true" information was that it would take only six days ("five sleeps") to reach their Nez Percé people on the other side of those tremendous mountains. Perhaps if the young Nez Percé had gone along that might have been true, but, as things happened it took the Expedition eleven days to make the crossing, and it was a nightmarish and hungry time for the men.

The Weippe Prairie where the Expedition encountered the Nez Perce. Photo courtesy Patricia Hastings.

The People

When Captain Clark, and then two days later, Captain Lewis and his men came down out of the mountains into Nez Perce country, they walked into an expansive, grassy plain that is now called Weippe Prairie, and met the Nez Percé. (Nez is pronounced in English as it looks. Percé rhymes with nurse.) They were a Shahaptian speaking, plateau people living in central Idaho, northern Oregon and southeastern Washington. They called themselves "the People" or the Neemeepoo. Lewis and Clark called them the Chopunnish, and they were also known as the "stuck noses" because of their custom to pierce the soft bone between the nostrils of their nose (the septum) for ornaments. The sign language gesture for them is an extended finger traveling under the nose. Early French trappers named them Nez Percé, which translates pierced nose. Both Captains made note of their ornaments. Captain Clark, May 7, 1806, *"The ornaments worn by the Choppunish are, in their noses a single shell of wampon. the pirl and beads are suspended from the ears...."*

Their land or territory is a study in contrasts; the barren Columbian plain diverges into fringed foothills and wooded mountains, with grassy prairies, glades, and winding rivers. The Nez Percé lived in villages along the Clearwater, Salmon, Snake, Columbia Rivers and their tributaries, which were all very productive water for fish. The rivers produced an incredible amount of salmon, perhaps more than any other place in the world. The Nez Percé, living nearby, consumed copious amounts of the salmon; nearly half their diet was salmon. They preserved it through drying and smoking, and then packed and stored it for use throughout the year. To supplement their rich salmon diet, the men hunted for wild game; deer, elk, bear, etc., and the eastern Nez Percé traveled over the mountains to the plains to take the buffalo.

Their land was fertile and beautiful and they were grateful for the wild, natural beauty of the earth. The People thanked the powerful spirit forces for their gifts by means of ritual ceremonies to mother earth. But, their oral tradition says there was more than just honoring the land and forces. It was knowing that every living thing was placed here by the Creator, and we all are part of a sacred relationship....

The land of the Nez Percé was rich with edible roots, vegetable foods, and berries. The women had long come to Weippe Prairie, to dig and prepare the rich onion-like, camas root, which Captain Lewis called "quamash," and Sergeant Whitehouse called the "wild potato." The camas was steamed, baked, and then smashed and pounded into meal, which was ultimately made into a bread-like cake, and then packed and stored for future use. (It was made into a porridge if eaten fresh.) The bread-cake was a staple food in the Nez Percé diet, along with dried salmon and wild berries, such as chokecherries, huckleberries, strawberries, gooseberries, serviceberries, etc., which were sun dried and stored. Other edible roots prepared by the women were kouse, bitterroots, wild carrot and celery, carum and others. Captain Lewis said, "The noise of their women pounding roots reminds me of the noise of a nail factory."

When the starving Explorers stumbled into the Nez Percé village, the people generously and possibly somewhat nervously, fed the hungry men. Captain Clark remarked, "There was both fear and pleasure in their eyes." For most of the Indians crowding around the explorers it was their first association with whites. They must have wondered who they were, where had they come from, and what they were doing. Nez Percé oral tradition says there was discussion about the bearded, starved, "fish-eyed" men. Some of the older men were suspicious and wanted to kill them. With a bit of guile, that might have been not too difficult, given the exhausted and weakened physical state they were in, plus the dire dysentery and other digestive disorders they were suffering after eating a couple of meals of camas and dried fish. A couple of men were already lying on the side of the road, moaning. Nez Percé tradition tells us that an elderly, respected woman, Wetxuwiss, told the elders to do the "soyapa," or white men no harm. She had met the whites while she was far from her homeland, kidnapped and in captivity by another tribe, and knew the soyapa to be friendly and considerate people. They had been helpful when she sought to find her way home. (Wetxuwiss's name means "the Person Who Returned Home. It is believed that she met a Nez Perce hunting expedition on the plains of Montana through news related to her by their allies, the Crows.)1. She told the elders the white men meant no harm and should be treated well. Her story impressed the older men, and the Neemeepoo befriended the Expedition and helped them.

Horsing Around

The Nez Percé had an incredible number of horses. Captain Lewis wrote, *"fifty, sixty, a hundred head is not unusual for an individual to possess, "*and they were fine horses too. Captain Lewis adds, *"It astonished me to see the order of their horses at this season of the year when I know they*

COLOR SECTION

The Corps of Discovery
still rides the Nez Perce Trail

Jean Clary

Artist Jean Clary of Stevensville, Montana, who also happens to be one of The Discovery Writers of that community who have written a number of books about the Lewis and Clark Expedition's experiences set in Montana, created this powerful watercolor "The Corps of Discovery Still Rides The Nez Perce Trail" after a research trip to the area regarding this book. Please see her story about that experience on Page 157 under the title "A Personal Journey." Photo courtesy Dale A. Burk.

A re-enactment at the Travelers' Rest site in 2002 by the Travelers' Rest Chapter of the Lewis and Clark Trail Heritage Foundation provided insight into what the encampment might have looked like. In photo are (from left), Tom Lukomski, George Knapp, George Truett, Chuck Sundstrom, Mike Wallace, and Ritchie Doyle. Photo courtesy Mary and Bruce Burk of the Lolo Peak News.

This hand-colored engraving by Alexander Wilson features three species of birds common in the Bitterroot Valley of Montana — the Western Tanager (formerly Louisiana Tanager), Lewis' Woodpecker, and the Clark's Nutcracker (formerly the Clark's Crow). The latter two species were named for Captains Meriwether Lewis and William Clark. Wilson rendered these images for a book published in 1808-14 titled "American Ornithology" using the very specimens collected by the Expedition on their return journey. A print of this owned by Robert Petty of Hamilton, Montana, can be viewed at the Ravalli County Museum in that city. Photo courtesy Dale A. Burk

The actual campsite at Travelers' Rest in a photo taken by the Travelers' Rest Preservation and Heritage Association in September, the same time of year that the Expedition first used the site in 1805. Photo courtesy Loren Flynn.

The camas in full bloom at Packer Meadow. This beautiful flower, most often referred to as the "quamash" in the journals, was an important source of food to the Native Americans. Photos courtesy Patricia Hastings.

On September 9, 1805, Captain Meriwether Lewis wrote in his journals regarding the stream we now call Lolo Creek these words: "We called this Creek Travellers rest ... a fine bould clear runing stream." This photo taken at the campsite shows it to still be a fine, clear-running stream. Photo courtesy Jeanne O'Neill.

The acquisition of good horses from the Salish during their encounter with this Native American group at Camp Creek in the upper reaches of the Bitterroot River enabled the Expedition to ultimately succeed in its crossing of the "awesome" Bitterroot Mountains. Here we show a re-enactment of the journey near Travelers' Rest involving Frank Castanza on the horse at left and Rick Hurst. Photo courtesy Don Merwin.

This drawing by Gustav Sohon titled "Entrance to The Rocky Mountains. By the Lou Lou Fork" is believed to be the oldest known artistic depiction of the area in which Travelers' Rest is located. It was published in 1860 as one of a series of drawings Sohon did for Isaac I. Stevens' "Narrative and Final Report of Explorations and Surveys for a Railroad Route From the Mississippi River to the Pacific Ocean," Vol. 12, Book 1, 1st Session (1860) Serial 1054. The Travelers' Rest site is at the far right of the scene, along Lolo Creek. Courtesy K. Ross Toole Archives, University of Montana. Photo courtesy Dale A. Burk.

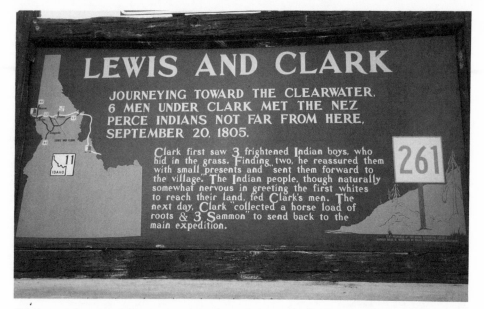

This sign along the Weippe Prairie acknowledges a shared history of the area from the 1805 encounter. Photo courtesy Patricia Hastings.

have wintered on dry grass of this plains and at the same time rode with great severity… I do not see a single horse which could be deemed poor and many are as fat as seals." The well- watered, grassy foothills, plateaus, and meadows with protein rich bunch grass in Nez Percé country were excellent for keeping horses. Nestling valleys and willow groves offered protection from wind and weather. Mountains, rock formations, sheers and chasms, presented natural obstructions and frustrated straying, giving the animals open range as home throughout the year.

In addition to a favorable environment, the Nez Percé bred their stock selectively. They might have been the only Indian nation to pursue that practice. At any rate, their horses were superior, showing as large, active, well-formed animals, unlike the homely, small- statured horses of the northern plains. The spotted horse was first noticed in the west among the Nez Percé. Early French trappers called them simply, "the Nez Percé Horse," later they became known as the Appaloosa. The Indians used them to parade during ceremonies and celebrations as showy horses for flashy exhibition.

Captain Lewis complained about "cuts" some of his horses received from aggressive stallions. Some of the horses had become so wild the Corps had to build a "make-shift wall" to hold them. The Indians could catch them by throwing a lasso around their necks. Ordinarily the men of the Corps had great difficulty taking the horses when needed, and it was decided some of the stallions had to be gelded (castrated). A Nez Percé steps in to show how they performed the procedure, and of course, the Captains compared the convalescence and recovery of the horses operated on by the Nez Percé with those done by the Expedition's men. Captain Lewis preferred the Indian way. He said, "Those cut by Indians get well much sooner and do not swell nor appear to suffer as much as those cut the common way."

Horses were used for barter and trade for items such as tools, foodstuffs, buffalo robes, ornaments, and objects of utility – which the Nez Percé seemed to prefer over baubles when trading with Lewis and Clark. One horse would command several items in trade, (depending on which items of course.) In the Indian economy the Nez Percé were wealthy. Horses were used in barter as money, and the Nez Percé had plenty of horses.

Both men and women were excellent riders. The Corps was astonished to see the Indians ride down the steep hills at full speed, sending arrows dead to the mark. The down side of their aggressive riding, however, was that the hard riding wounded the backs of their horses. Sometimes the Nez Percé rode their horses without saddles, which were dressed pads stuffed with mountain goat hair. The stirrups were wooden, and the bridle was usually a hair rope, tied with both ends to the under jaw of the horse. The pads *did not prevent the weight of the rider pressing immediately on the backbone and weathers of the horse,"* according to Captain Lewis. Nez Percé women began to bead-decorate the bridle and their saddle blankets, which they used both under and on the saddle. The women used horses to assist them in transporting needed items over harsh, rugged terrain. They devised packs, gear and techniques for the animals to haul firewood, children, berry- loads, the sick, etc., and when whole families moved to the "quamash" prairie for root collecting and nearby fishing, the horses hauled everything back and forth. When the women traveled without men, dogs were taken, no matter how short the distance. Their sense of smell would alert women to marauding animals, or other hostilities. Sometimes the dogs would also help transport materials, if needed.

The Nez Percé were horse people by the middle of the Eighteenth Century, no longer walking up steep sides of rocky benches and foot-hills to forage and hunt. Horses enabled the Neemeepoo to easily travel east over the Bitterroot Mountains to buffalo country, and along with the buffalo meat, they brought back knowledge of the plains culture, and incorporated parts of it into their Columbian plateau heritage: the tepee, buffalo robe, and others. Broken Arm, a Nez Percé Chief, had a large conical lodge of leather erected for Lewis and Clark's reception when they returned to the Clearwater area to retrieve the Expedition's horses that wintered there, and to find guides to lead them across the Bitterroot Mountains. The chief invited the Explorers to make the lodge their home while with him. Broken Arm's (or Tumachemootool, his Shahaptian name) "village consisted of one long house, which was one hundred fifty feet in length, and built in the usual form of stick-mats and dry grass", Captain Lewis, May, 1806. They were called mat-houses although their frames were timber and poles. The mats covering the wooden frame were made of cured hemp, dogbane, or cattail, scraped and split, braided into long strands, and then sewn together. Broken Arm's long mat-house contained "twenty-four fires and double that number of families...." The cooking fires were staggered in a long row down the central corridor of the long mat house with each fire servicing two families. The houses were lengthened to accommodate more families as the village grew.

Captain Clark described the Chopunnish or Nez Percé as, *"darker than the Tushapaws (Salish) I have seen...their dress is similar, with more beads, white and blue principally, brass and copper in different forms, shells, wear their hair in the same way. They are large portly men. Small women and handsome featured."*

For their ankle-length dresses the women seemed to prefer soft sheepskin, and used it for baby clothing also. Most of the clothing for men, shirts, leggings, moccasins, and armor were processed from elk skins. Mountain sheepskin processed with the hair was used for robes and some family clothing. Later, they took on some of the plain's dress, wearing paint-designed shirts with plain's decoration and embroidery. But, the Nez Percé held on to their traditional way of life: salmon fishing, camas, foraging, local hunting, and ceremonies until they were overwhelmed by whites and the gold rush.

Hospitality

The Nez Percé and the Corps of Discovery were on friendly terms, and spent time together socially: they shared meals, camped, counciled, bartered, smoked, foot-raced, horse-raced, danced to Pierre Cruzatte's fiddle music, hold shooting matches (Captain Lewis won; 2 marks@ 220 ft. No wonder he had so many friends. And, the Neemeepoo were astounded at the gun's distance and accuracy. Aah Ho.) They played games, Prisoner's Base and pitched quoites. On the political front, Captain Lewis gave the Nez Percé chiefs flags, counsel, and medals with likenesses of Jefferson and Washington; The Nez Percé gave them elegant horses and colts to signify their respect and willingness to attend to the Explorers advice. (But it was the Nez Percé Council's job to decide about the new American government's offers and plans, and they were wary.) On the diet front, the Nez Percé gave the Explorers fat horses for meat to supplement their diet of roots.

Nez Percé chiefs were both hospitable and helpful:

•Red Grizzly Bear told the Explorers whenever they were in want of meat, to kill "any of his horses."

•The elderly Twisted Hair (not a chief) drew a map of the river systems of the Columbia drainage on white elk skin for the Captains; was winter caretaker of their horses; interpreter, liaison, and guide to Columbia Falls.

Another sign commemorates the historic initial meeting of the Lewis and Clark Expedition with the friendly Nez Perce at Weippe Prairie on September 20, 1805. Photo courtesy Patricia Hastings.

•Broken Arm's immediate response of two fat horses for the fatigued and hungry Expedition upon their reentry into the Clearwater region brought this response from Captain Lewis on May 10, 1806. *"In short be it spoken to their immortal honor it is the only act which deserves the appellation of hospitality which we have witnessed in this quarter."*

•And, Chief Neeshneparkkeook (or Cut Nose) sent his brother and two other respected young men of their nation) to guide the Expedition over the Bitterroot Mountains.

Admirable Pilots

The Explorers were not looking forward to another face-off with the Bitterroot Mountains. They still had not forgotten the suffering of the journey the previous fall, but the return trip over the daunting Behemoths was not a repeat nightmare of the first crossing. No one had cleaned up the fallen logs or cleared out the thickets. The ledges were still as sharp and narrow, and it was still the most rugged place of their journey, but this time it worked better.

The Nez Percé returned all of the Expedition's horses that had wintered with them on the plains, and Captain Lewis said most of them were in excellent condition. There was no finer occurrence for the Corps. The men were all pretty bedraggled, and had almost nothing left to barter, how could they have acquired new horses if needed? They were down to trading buttons off their jackets. With the horses picked up along the Columbia River, they would have enough to make the passage over the mountains without lugging gear and equipment themselves.

All of the men in the Expedition did as much trading with the Nez Percé as possible for dried food items. Captain Lewis said he believed each man had enough provisions to get them over the mountains after Captain Clark and five men came back from the Indian village with a sizable supply of goods. What Lewis said turned out to be true because Sergeant Patrick Gass wrote two days before the completed journey to Travelers' Rest, *"We still have a good stock of roots, which we pound and make a thick soup of, that eats well."* Fishing and hunting were both good enough to add a little extra nutrition and well being for the men of the Expedition most of the time.

There were three young Nez Percé guides for the return crossing of the Bitterroots. Captain Lewis thought, *"They were men of good character and much respected by their nation."* Considering the time period, available technology and equipment, and the conditions, (there was still seven feet of snow in parts of the mountains) the young guides, in today's parlance, could be considered on-the-trail professionals. They knew the ins and outs of their heritage trail. They had probably begun crossing the Old Road to the Buffalo in a cradleboard swinging from the horn of their mother's saddle as their village proceeded to hunting grounds on the Great Plains. It must have struck Captain Lewis as astoundingly competent when coming out of snow pack onto a dry patch to find a worn path. He wrote, *These fellows are most admirable pilots, we find the road whenever the snow has disappeared though it be only for a few hundred paces.* The Expedition tried crossing the mountains alone, without guides, before snow-melt, against advice, and were forced to retreat. (The only retreat of the entire journey.)

"I doubt whether we who had once passed (the mountains) could find our way to Travellers rest...." Captain Lewis wrote on June of 1806. The Nez Perce guides led the Expedition to shelter from the weather. *"We got in the evening to the side of the hill where snow was gone; and there was very good grass for our horses,"* Sergeant Gass wrote on June 26, 1806.

Advice from the Nez Percé led the Explorers to camp early one afternoon because the heavily packed horses were tired. The young guides told them, better to let the horses rest because good grass was too far away to reach before the following day. Talking the matter over the Captains probably decided what the guides said was true, the young men certainly had a track record, anyway, they settled there for the night. The next day the horses ate well.

With as much ease as the mountains, weather and equipment would allow, in seven days ("six sleeps") the Nez Percé led the men to Travelers' Rest, where they rested and prepared for the next part of their journey. In two days they set off. This time they would head in different directions for different missions:

•Captain Clark, with eighteen men, Sacajawea, Pomp, York, and Charbonneau, headed south. He would find what is today Bozeman Pass while heading for exploration of the Yellowstone River.

•Captain Lewis rode away from Travelers' Rest with nine men, five Nez Perce, and seventeen horses, headed for the Continental Divide at the headwaters of the Blackfoot River near Lincoln, Montana, and then on to explore the Marias River in Blackfoot territory.

The divided party would meet at the confluence of the Missouri and Yellowstone Rivers in one month, homeward bound.

Chapter 7

SPLITTING THE PARTY

Having passed the confluence of two major rivers on the Upper Missouri on their way west and with only a brief time to explore each, Captains Lewis and Clark had many unanswered questions. Where were the headwaters of the Yellowstone and Marias Rivers? Did the Marias extend above the 49th parallel? What about the potential for fur trade along these routes? Were there unknown indian tribes along these water sheds? Could one of the tributaries be part of the Northwest Passage – the route of President Jefferson's dreams?

Jefferson had asked them to explore the headwaters of the Missouri and to establish the northern most reaches of the same. They were to find the most direct navigable route to the Pacific Ocean, as well. Although the Corps of Discovery had gleaned much valuable information at Mandan from fur traders and indians, there were surprises, especially, geographical.

Members of the party were shocked in 1805 when they came upon the Marias River. How could such a large tributary of the Missouri have gone unmentioned? The Indians and fur traders must to have known about it? Another glaring example was the Rocky Mountain Range. Using the maps supplied by President Jefferson and information gathered at Fort Mandan, they were expecting to find a narrow range broken occasionally by open plains. Captain Lewis was taken back by the extent of the Rockies. There was a possibility the information had been provided but was lost in one of the many translations some of which were sign language.

Natural curiosity made these explorers want to see more of this newly acquired territory. Many questions remained unanswered. Therefore, plans were made well in advance of July 3, 1806, to split the party at Travelers' Rest on their return trip – enabling more exploration.

On February 14, 1806, at Fort Clatsop, Captain Clark completed his map of the area extending from Fort Mandan to the Pacific Coast. On viewing the finished product, both captains agreed they had taken the most direct route from the Missouri to the Pacific Ocean with the exception of the Indian short-cut extending from the great falls of the Missouri River to Travelers' Rest. They decided they would take every opportunity possible to confirm this conclusion.

Captain Clark spent hours and possibly days calculating distances from key points along the route. The Travelers' Rest campsite was one of these key positions. This location was certainly an important geographical point in the mind of the Expedition's cartographer.

While the captains' decision to split the party is sometimes questioned, they were certain to have known the risk and, for them, the benefits

A view of the campsite at Travelers' Rest, looking east. The fire pit for cooking was located in the foreground and the latrine in the distance, adjacent to the line of trees at the right. Photo courtesy Patricia Hastings.

outweighed the dangers. Although little was recorded in the journals regarding the separation, the prospects of potential tragedy must have weighed heavily on the captains' minds as they finalized plans and prepared to part.

Before they were reunited at the mouth of the Yellowstone River, they would split into five smaller parties. Each small party would have horses, guns and other valuable items making them an easy prize for indian war parties. While the threat of starvation was behind, other dangers lay ahead. There were grizzlies, rattlesnakes, possible injuries, drownings, and sickness to mention a few. In the spring of 1805, Captain Lewis wrote, *"as I have always held it a crime to anticipate evils I will believe it a good and comfortable road untill I am compelled to believe differently."* With this as his motto, he would venture the risk.

July 3, 1806 – The day had arrived to set in motion a plan to confirm, to the best of their ability, what they believed to be true. The party would

On July 3, 1806, Captain Lewis and his party crossed the broad Clark Fork River upriver of where the Kona Ranch Bridge is today. The party then camped at the junction of Grant Creek and the Clark Fork. At a compass bearing of N 75 ° E, the party headed eastward toward Hell's Canyon the next morning. Photo courtesy Patricia Hastings.

split. Captain Lewis would take nine men and seventeen horses north, cross the Clark's (Clark Fork) River and proceed up the Nez Perce Trail (road to the buffalo) along the Blackfoot River to the Continental Divide. From there, his party would drop down to the Medicine (Sun) River and follow it to the White Bear Islands near the great falls of the Missouri. The nine men accompanying Captain Lewis were Sergeant Gass and Privates Joseph and Reuben Field, William Werner, Robert Frazier, John Thompson, Silas Goodrich, Hugh McNeal, and an interpreter, George Drouillard (Drewyer). Once they were at the falls, they would split a second time. After opening the cache, Captain Lewis would take six men to explore the Marias while three others remained at White Bear Island.

While awaiting the arrival of a detachment of Captain Clark's party, under the command of Sergeant Ordway, these three men were to prepare the 'wagons' for portaging the falls. Once the portage was complete, Sergeant Ordway, along with twelve men, would retrieve items left in the upper cache near the mouth of Belt Creek and then proceed downriver to Camp Decision.

Here, at the mouth of the Marias, again, they were to gather items

Pompey's Pillar along the Yellowstone River in southeastern Montana, where Captain William Clark carved his initials into the rock on July 25, 1806, on the party's way back to St. Louis. The pillar is named for Sacajawea's son, Pompey Charbonneau, "Little Pomp". Photo courtesy Jessica Ladd Cook.

cached, pick up Captain Lewis and his party and continue east on the Missouri to rejoin Captain Clark's party at the confluence of the Yellowstone River.

Meanwhile, Captain Clark would take the remainder of the party south along the Flathead (Bitterroot) River to the 1805 Salish camp (at Ross' Hole) where he was to take a new route via the southern Nee Mee Poo Trail over the Continental Divide (Gibbon's Pass) to Camp Fortunate at the headwaters of the Beaverhead River. After opening the cache there, collecting items and retrieving canoes stored there for more than ten months, Sergeant Ordway would take several men in canoes down the Jefferson River while Captain Clark and other members of the party traveled overland with the horses, eventually, meeting Ordway at the Three Forks of the Missouri. Once there, Sergeant Ordway and nine men would head north on the Missouri to White Bear Island where they were to join Captain Lewis' detachment for the portage around the falls.

While Sergeant Ordway's party made their way down the Missouri, Captain Clark, ten men, Sacagawea and baby Pomp, would head east to explore the Yellowstone River. After crossing into the Yellowstone drainage, they were to construct canoes. Captain Clark, seven men, Sacagawea, and baby Pomp, would travel east via the river while Sergeant Pryor and two privates were to take the horses overland to Fort Mandan. After leaving most of the horses at the fort, Sergeant Pryor's detachment was to continue to the Assiniboine River in present day Manitoba, with a letter for Hugh Heney, a British fur trader.

This letter, composed by Captain Lewis at Travelers' Rest on July 2, 1806, offered Mr. Heney a job working as an Indian agent with the Sioux to establish an American trade empire. Mr. Heney, held in high regard by the Sioux, especially the Teton Sioux with whom the Corps of Discovery had a confrontation on their trip west, was asked by Captain Lewis to persuade the Indians, now United States citizens, to send a delegation to Washington.

Wanting the Sioux to trade through St. Louis rather than with the British through Canada and given their own experience with the Teton Sioux, they realized the potential for conflict and control of trade goods moving up and down the Missouri River. It was important to negotiate a treaty as soon as possible.

After exploring the Yellowstone River basin, Captain Clark was to wait at the mouth of the Yellowstone for the arrival of Captain Lewis' party before continuing on to St. Louis.

Chapter 8

AFTER LEWIS & CLARK

Trappers for the Hudson's Bay Company were plying the waters and forests of the Lolo Creek Area by 1809-1810. In 1812 David Thompson, noted geographer and employee of the North West Fur Company, climbed present-day Mount Jumbo and surveyed the Missoula Valley.

The Source of Lolo Creek's Name

A French trapper named Lawrence, known to have been in contact with Thompson, settled in the Lolo Creek area. Tradition claims that there was no "r" sound in the Native American language , but the Indians replaced "r" with "l"and Lawrence became Lou Lou, then Lo Lo. Whatever, the old fur trapper's name is now memorialized in Lolo Canyon, Lolo Creek, Lolo Peak, Lolo Pass, Lolo Trail, Lolo Hot Springs, Lolo National Forest and the small community of Lolo which incorporates Travelers' Rest.

Great imagination in choosing names! By all accounts Lawrence and his Nez Perce wife were the first settlers in the area, and he is buried here. The search for his grave continues.

It is said that in 1831 Hudson's Bay Company trader John Work, with fifty to sixty Scotch and French trappers and numerous Indian men, women and children, passed over Lolo Trail with great difficulty, almost being lost on the treacherous snowy passage. By 1845 most of the beaver had been trapped out, and the trappers made way for the prospectors searching for their bonanza which apparently eluded them. However, a gold mine, the Chickman, supposedly yielded $25,000 and a copper mine existed from 1898 to 1914.

In 1846 the Oregon Treaty defined the 49th parallel as the boundary between the United States and Britain. The Oregon Territory included the Lolo-Missoula area. Transportation here was, for the most part, along the Indian trails through the Bitterroot Valley and north to Missoula and beyond. Still, the third road of the Indian "hub," the one west through the Lolo Canyon eluded those who sought it. In 1854 Lieutenant John Mullan, who surveyed the Mullan Road from Walla Walla, Washington, to Fort Benton, Montana, explored the Canyon to find a possible railroad route. However, his experience paralleled that of Lewis and Clark. After eleven days he and his men emerged claiming that it was an extremely difficult route. Gold-seeking miners pressed for a wagon road over Lolo and a survey was made, but no road was built. By 1888 a barely passable road did exist to Lolo Hot Springs but was not upgraded to gravel until 1935. Meanwhile, a stagecoach, the Missoula-Fort Owen, carried passengers and freight up the Bitterroot Valley, with stage stops including Lolo along the way

---

An Earlier Description of The Town of Lolo
"LOLO (Ind, muddy water, (3,198 alt. 102 pop.) Is made up of a store, a beer hall, a service station, and a few houses and tourist cabins." – WPA Guide to 1930's Montana.

The Northern Pacific Railroad arrived in Missoula in 1883; a Bitterroot spur line reached Lolo in 1889. Sawmills cropped up around the valley feeding ties to the railroads and lumber to the insatiable appetite of the Butte mines. In 1909 a railroad war ensued when the Northern Pacific and Union Pacific railroads vied against one another to complete a railroad survey through Lolo Canyon. Up to twenty-one hundred men were reported to be working in the Canyon bringing a short-lived boom to Lolo. They completed the survey for "The Clearwater Railroad," which was never built. Like Lieutenant John Mullan before them, the railroad managers concluded that building a railroad was not feasible. Although Native Americans had traveled back and forth on their "road to the buffalo" through Lolo Canyon for centuries, not until 1962 were builders able to complete the Lewis and Clark Highway (U.S. Highway 12) connecting Lolo with Lewiston, Idaho. However, the "hub" is still there. Where Indian trails once converged at an ancient campsite Lewis and Clark named Travelers' Rest, two United States

Highways, 93 and 12, now intersect at the crossroads of the place the Indians called Lolo.

The Homestead Act of 1862 opened up the area to more settlers. Enter John Delaney, a farsighted Irish immigrant, who arrived in 1865, looked at the intersection where the trail west "up Lolo Creek" intersected with the mainstream through the Bitterroot Valley and filed for a homestead at the crossroads. In 1885 Delaney received his patent and proceeded to build a livery stable, a blacksmith shop, a saloon and a mercantile store with an upstairs dance hall. The Delaney establishments became the nucleus of the community of Lolo. A school soon followed with forty students attending in 1890.

The Tick Scare

"Spotted Fever" is a sometimes fatal disease carried by wood ticks. A particularly virulent strain invaded the Bitterroot in the early 1900's and infested the Lolo Canyon. Almost every area family mourned the loss of a loved one to this disease, but not until Dr. Howard T. Ricketts of the U.S. Public Health Service researched spotted fever was the wood tick found to be the vector of the causative organism. Sheep and small rodents were the hosts. A control program ensued which included eradicating small rodents and dipping the sheep in an arsenic based solution which killed the ticks. Researchers developed a vaccine, but only after several died of the disease during their research. Tick disease is still a threat, but with early diagnosis and treatment, fatalities seldom occur.

The little community of Lolo proceeded to grow through the Twentieth Century like most small settlements in western Montana. Prohibition, in force from 1919 until 1933, brought bootlegging into the valley, where the clear soft mountain water made tasty moonshine The automobile changed the transportation scene resulting in better roads and paved highways. Highway 12 became the preferred road for truckers hauling freight to the port at Lewiston, Idaho, while commercial establishments continued to sprout up around the crossroads. Lolo has now developed into a bedroom community for Missoula, a movement which accelerated when Hwy. 93 , between Lolo and Missoula, was expanded to a four lane thoroughfare.

As more people relocate into the Bitterroot Valley and the Missoula area , land developers are building subdivisions to accommodate a swelling population of 3,388 according to the U.S. census of 2000, the new residents of Lolo. The surrounding hills are dotted with new homes, some of which are labeled "trophy houses," clinging to the hillsides. Meanwhile, Lolo residents are asking the big question. Should Lolo incorporate as a town or risk the possibility of being annexed by the bigger, expanding city of Missoula, which is slowly creeping southward? In the words of the late historian, K. Ross Toole, "the winds of change are blowing over Montana." Those winds still blow and, like it or not, Lolo is in their path.

A portion of the original Lolo Trail at Howard Creek on the Lolo National Forest. Photo courtesy Patricia Hastings.

Chapter 9

ADDITIONAL ASPECTS OF THE TRAVELERS' REST STORY

The saga of Travelers' Rest is inescapably linked to the area's entire history. It is an ongoing story, one like that of the Travelers' Rest site itself – rooted deep in history and yet moving ahead, pulsating, alive. Consequently, the stories that follow in this chapter provide additional insight into the story of this historic locale with, always, a link to the place we call Travelers' Rest.

PAT & ERNIE DESCHAMPS

What odds would a gambler give that a little nondescript parcel of land bordering Lolo Creek in western Montana, with no known historical past of significance, would remain untouched for two hundred years while all about it neighboring land was plowed, irrigated, farmed, grazed, subdivided, bought and sold, and that the discovery of the history of this little parcel of land would pitch its unknowing owners into the swirl of interest surrounding the bicentennial of the famous Lewis and Clark Expedition? Certainly not the owners, Pat and Ernie Deschamps, address, 6550 Mormon Creek Road, Lolo, Montana, 59847.

One spring morning in 1996 Pat Deschamps answered a telephone call that forever changed her's and Ernie's quiet life in Lolo. Chuck Sundstrom, president of the local chapter of the Lewis and Clark Trail Heritage Foundation, informed the surprised couple that they were living on what was believed to be the actual campsite of the Lewis and Clark Expedition

– Travelers' Rest Creek – named by Meriwether Lewis on September 9, 1805. Very soon, Pat and Ernie found themselves being interviewed and photographed for leading newspapers. Crowds of people came to their door, and, finally, they would sell and leave their home of more than thirty years.

Pat and Ernie are Montana natives who grew up in the small town of Alberton, married and lived in Missoula's Orchard Homes area until 1968, when they bought farmland with a house in the little undeveloped community of Lolo. Here they reared their two children, Cathy and Mike, and opened their home to a foster child. A few animals, horses, sheep, cattle and dogs shared the pasture while Ernie worked for the railroad and farmed. The little house was a real "fixer upper," a challenge for Ernie and Pat. But soon the "fixer upper" became a tidy, attractive white cottage.

"So Ernie, why didn't you ever plow that bottomland of yours behind your house?" he was asked.

"If we could have afforded it, we'd have wrecked the whole thing. We never got enough money ahead to build the fish pond I wanted," he replied.

Instead, Ernie, an up-front Montanan and Pat, a genuine Montana homemaker, unknowingly preserved this historical legacy for which they have received acclaim and awards for their stewardship, and for their willingness to put this property in the hands of those who would preserve

Ernie and Pat Deschamps. Photo courtesy Patricia Hastings.

rather than capitalize or exploit the fact for personal gain.

Shock, surprise and what now? Historians, both professional and amateur, scientists, authors, archeologists, state and local officials, botanists from Philadelphia, Native Americans, school children and their teachers, all arrived at the little white house on Mormon Creek Road, inquiring, observing. "Some were curious," Pat noted, "Some were reverent." The late Stephen Ambrose had tears in his eyes as he stood on the campsite in the footsteps of Meriwether Lewis and his companions, whom Ambrose wrote of in his book, *"Undaunted Courage."*

"The 'HI' sign on their fence rather than the customary 'NO TRESPASSING' sign has made Pat and Ernie remarkable," Francis Weigand, friend and member of the local chapter of the Lewis and Clark Heritage Trail Foundation. Pat treasures the signed guest books and pictures of her visitors. No matter how many callers arrived at their door, Pat and Ernie kept jars filled with red licorice sticks beside the guest book with a placard "sign and take a vine."

Meanwhile, the Deschamps held tight waiting to see what would happen to them and the property. Three years of negotiations passed before a private buyer offered to purchase the property provided it would go into public ownership and that it would sell for appraised market value only, no historical value allowed – also that it would pass into ownership where its

---

Living At Travelers' Rest

"As I look back on my childhood,

I wonder if the Expedition inspired me

to build that large tree house in the field.

If I had only known who stood there before I arrived,

It would have been much more special to me.

I can only tell you,

It is a place that calms your heart,

a place that brings peace to your soul,

a place where beloved pets lie in eternal rest.

It should remain just as it is forever."

Cathy Deschamps

---

legacy would be preserved for all generations of Americans. On March 20, 2001, transactions completed, the Deschamps property became Travelers' Rest State Park. Pat and Ernie said goodbye to Lolo and to all that goes into the making and sustaining of home and family, of dreams and memories. However, life is good for them in their new residence in Florence just six miles from Lolo. Pat admits that she misses her home, but she and Ernie are pleased at seeing "people coming together, working for a common goal."

Meanwhile, all bets are off for those who might like to gamble regarding such things. Without knowing it Pat and Ernie beat the odds and enabled the preservation of one of America's most cherished historical sites – and upon learning that it could be done, they made sure the chance to preserve it was given to all coming generations of a nation enthralled with the Lewis & Clark Expedition.

THE TRAVELING TRUNK

"How can we save Travelers' Rest?" mused Chuck Sundstrom and George Knapp, amateur historians and dedicated enthusiasts of the Lewis and Clark Expedition, a number of years ago. "What can we do to catch the attention and educate people, especially children, about the Lewis and Clark Expedition in general and Travelers' Rest in particular? We need their help in saving the campsite."

"Show and tell, that's the answer." And the notion of a "Traveling Trunk" full of historical items related to the Lewis & Clark Expedition was born.

The Traveling Trunk is a unique and innovative way to personalize the Expedition and bring its story to children and adults in schools and meeting halls, even on tour buses. Chuck and George, members of the Travelers' Rest Chapter of the Lewis and Clark Trail Heritage Foundation, went on a search.

"We researched the Journals, visited museums, even the Smithsonian, haunted antique stores, attended rendevous', asked help from collectors, purchased what we could. Some items were donated and some were specially made."

Since 1990, George has been collecting bits and pieces of information in order to duplicate the costume of Captain Lewis. Every item in the traveling trunk is backed up by two written proofs of authenticity; weapons, tools, scientific instruments, medicines, camp equipment, clothing, presents for the Indians, etc. Consequently, Chuck, dressed as Meriwether Lewis, and George as William Clark, show and describe each item in the trunk. Chuck loads a rifle with a lead ball; George holds up a replica of the square wooden plate used by the Expedition and explains that the expression "square meal" originated here. Two types of moccasins are displayed, with patterns for each. A laptop desk, a quill pen and dry ink powder are popular items, as is a replica of Sacajawea's dress and the tomahawk made and donated by Hoot Gibson of Victor, Montana. A hands-on demonstration, starting fire with a flint, captivates the children. Questions pop up from the audience. Either George or Chuck readily answer from their depth of knowledge and research of the day to day life of the Expedition; how the members dressed, ate, hunted, doctored, observed, used scientific instruments of the time, and applied their frontier experience to survive.

The Traveling Trunk was launched March 6, 1996, at the Alberton school. How successful was it? Chuck and George, assisted by members of the Traveler's Rest Chapter, have presented the Trunk show to more than 23,000 people in Montana and Idaho in the last six years, often in schools where students are astonished to see the Captains Lewis and Clark bounding

George Knapp (left) and Chuck Sundstrom have taken their "Traveling Trunk" program about the Lewis and Clark Expedition to hundreds of classrooms, using authentic replicas of the tools and equipment used by the Corps of Discovery. Here they are with teacher Jodi Hunt during a presentation in her classroom at the Target Range School in Missoula, Montana. Photo courtesy Jeanne O'Neill.

up the stairs or scurrying along hallways. These two volunteers, faithful impersonators of the famous explorers, are dedicated to authenticity and to getting their story out. The Traveling Trunk is largely responsible for the enthusiasm and activity surrounding interest in the Lewis and Clark Expedition in the region. Chuck Sundstrom and George Knapp deserve the acclaim and appreciation they receive for helping to initiate the search for the true location of the Travelers' Rest site, for dedicating and volunteering their time and treasure to bring and to enliven the dramatic story of the Corps of Discovery. Recently, they donated the trunk and its contents for demonstrations at the newly formed Travelers' Rest State Park.

THE BITTERROOT VALLEY

"The Beautiful Bitterroot" valley is the ancestral home of the Salish Indians. At the request of the Indians, the "Blackrobes," Catholic Jesuit priests, established a mission at present-day Stevensville in 1841. The priests introduced the first agriculture, the first cattle, the first saw mill and flour mill in Montana. In 1850 the priests sold the mission to Major John Owen. This bill of sale was the first land conveyance in Montana. Major Owen

The Bitterroot Valley was the ancestral home of the Salish people. It was in the upper reaches of the Bitterroot, at the junction of Camp Creek and the East Fork of the Bitterroot River where an encampment of the Salish first encountered, and helped, the Lewis and Clark Expedition. Photo courtesy Dale A. Burk.

erected a nonmilitary trading fort, Fort Owen, that was the center of the little community that evolved around it, Stevensville, named for Washington Territorial Governor Isaac Stevens. In 1866 the Jesuits fathers returned to reestablish the St. Mary's Mission. Father Anthony Ravalli served there until his death in 1884. This remarkable man, artist, architect, inventor, builder, doctor, who built a blacksmith shop and pharmacy and cared for the sick, is memorialized in the name, Ravalli County, which was split off from Missoula County in 1893.

The Council Grove Treaty, 1855, provided that the Salish be removed to the Jocko Reservation in the Mission Valley. Many Indians left, but Chief Charlo and his band remained in the Bitterroot. A forged signature, misunderstandings, and the failure of the United States to live up to the treaty resulted in a political rift between the Salish chiefs. A forced trail of tears in 1891 managed to remove the remainder of these peaceful friends of the United States who boasted that they had never shed the blood of any American.

Settlers arrived to farm, ranch and raise dairy cattle, sheep and hogs. Marcus Daly, the Butte copper baron, pioneered horse raising and initiated the lumber industry to supply the voracious appetites of his Butte mines and smelters. Daly built his own town, Hamilton, the largest community in the valley, which ultimately became the county seat. When Montana experienced the gold rush, prospectors staked claims in the Bitterroot, but no bonanzas surfaced. The Apple Boom, 1910-1911, was a land scheme that lured eastern investors to the valley with promises of big money in apple orchards. Weather and competition from Washington State ended the apple boom, which resulted in ruin for many and big profits for the few. It is still commemorated by "Apple Days" celebration, sponsored by the Ravalli County Museum.

The Lee Metcalf National Wildlife Refuge just north of Stevensville honors the late U.S. Senator Lee Metcalf, a Stevensville native and a conservationist of national renown, who fought to save areas of the West and supported the establishment of the Selway-Bitterroot Wilderness which encompasses part of the Bitterroot Range bordering the valley

The clear free-flowing Bitterroot River, the easily available forest trails and creeks in the mountains, plus clean air invite recreationists to come and enjoy and lure retirees into staying. The ancient Indian trail along the Bitterroot River over which the Expedition passed is now covered over by U.S. Highway 93, a modern four lane highway. Ravalli County, population 39,000, one of the fastest growing counties in Montana, is experiencing the problems of growth. With no zoning in place, sprawl, and strip development are changing the rural pastoral scene along Highway 93. Still, in the words of Russ Lawrence in his book *Montana's Bitterroot Valley,* "the Bitterroot is paradise with a slow leak, difficult to plug.... It's rural nature, breathtaking scenery, pristine river and small town character are slowly diminishing while the worst of the rest of the world occasionally leaks in...Yet it remains a highly desirable place to live, that offers a challenge with every opportunity and a reward for every hardship."

CELESTIAL READINGS
'Navigating' to the Pacific Ocean

In President Thomas Jefferson's commissioning the exploration of the Louisiana Purchase and beyond, he directed Captains Lewis and Clark to survey to the best of their ability, the region through which they would travel. Captain Lewis was personally instructed to purchase the scientific instruments necessary for the tasks.

President Jefferson arranged to have fellow members and friends of the American Philosophical Society expand the captain's knowledge regarding the use of equipment and the collection of data necessary to determine points of longitude and latitude along the route. One of these men was Andrew Ellicott, the nation's leading astronomer and therefore an expert in making celestial observations. The instruments most commonly used were the octant and the sextant. As personal secretary to the president, Captain Lewis had access to the president's instruments and library. He spent hours reading and practicing with the octant and sextant. Of the several books Captain Lewis carried on the expedition, there were at least two related to celestial readings. They were *A Practical Introduction to Spheres and Nautical Astronomy* and *The Nautical Almanac and Astronomical Ephemeris.* In addition to the reference books he carried on the expedition, there were a number of charts and tables necessary for fixing geographic locations. With the books, charts, instruments and instruction he received, Captain Lewis was equipped to carry out the president's requests.

Both triangular in shape, the octant was made of wood and brass and the sextant was brass. Because it was all metal, the sextant was regarded as the superior instrument. The 'triangle' consisted of two arms connected to a graduated arc at the bottom. The arc on the octant was forty five degrees (one eighth of a circle) and the sextant sixty degrees (one sixth of a circle).

Each had a movable arm hinged at the apex, a telescope (sight), shades and two mirrors. One mirror called the index glass was attached to the moveable or index arm and the other, half mirror and half glass, was attached to the arm opposite the sight. The telescope functioned to give definition to the horizon. Some octants had an additional lens attached to the stationery arm which was used when the view of the horizon was blocked or poorly defined. This extra lens enabled the viewer to sight in the opposite horizon. Both instruments were made to measure the angular distances between two objects such as the sun or a star and the horizon or they could be used to measure the angular distances between celestial bodies.

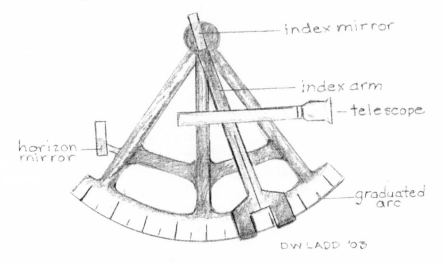

To use an octant or sextant, the observer held the instrument in a vertical position with the apex pointing straight upward. Sighting through the telescope, the viewer looked at the horizon reflected in the horizon glass. He then moved the index arm until the image of the sun or star reflected by index glass touched the horizon line. The position of the moveable arm on the graduated arc gave the observer a reading in degrees of the sun's or star's elevation above the earth's horizon. Given this number, the viewer referred to astronomical charts to find his point of latitude.

Another method in which no charts are required, is to determine the angle of the North Star above the horizon. From any location in the Northern Hemisphere, this angle, measured in degrees, is equal to the degrees latitude of the point from which the observation was made. For instance, if the angle between the North Star and the horizon is 45°, then the latitude for that point is 45° North. The problem with this procedure is that the North Star is not always visible or bright enough.

In order for these instruments to work without additional apparatus, the view of the distant horizon must be unobstructed. While this was possible on large bodies of water or on open plains, treed and mountainous areas presented a problem. Therefore, the instruments used by the Expedition were equipped with an artificial horizon. They carried an octant, sextants and three different artificial horizons. One type of artificial horizon was a trough of mercury (the captains used water) sheltered by two angled pieces of glass to keep the wind from rippling the surface of the liquid. The liquid acted much like a mirror. Effective in bright light, this horizon enabled the observer to determine the angle between the sun and its image on the liquid. This angle was two times the sun's apparent altitude. Another artificial horizon used a wooden ball with an attached glass plate adjusted with a spirit level and platform. This method was employed in conditions of dim light. The third artificial horizon was an index mirror attached to a flat board adjusted by a spirit level and a platform. This one was also used in bright light.

After spending several weeks in training with the highly recognized scientist and surveyor, Major Ellicott, Captain Lewis secured the equipment and charts needed for celestial observations. Major Ellicott felt it would be impossible for the captain to make the necessary mathematical calculations to fix points of latitude and longitude in the field. He encouraged proficiency in the use of the instruments and stressed the importance of accuracy in every aspect of the observations.

In addition to the sextants and octant, the explorers needed an accurate time piece, a surveyors compass, a two pole chain, and a drafting set. The time piece chosen was an English made gold-cased chronometer or 'Arnold' clock. Unable to find a new one and with no time to order the chronometer from England, Captain Lewis purchased a used one in Philadelphia from clock maker, Thomas Parker. The clock was both expensive and fragile. The clock's balance wheel could easily be broken. To protect this valuable piece of equipment, Captain Lewis had Mr. Parker build a special wooden case with suspension pins. Having another watch maker clean and calibrate the clock, Captain Lewis set about ordering other necessary equipment. On May 31, 1803, the following items were ordered:

A spirit level
One parallel horizon glass
One case of plotting instruments
Four ounces of talc

A two pole chain

Five compasses (one silver plated pocket type, one brass boat compass, and three brass pocket types)

One magnet

A tangent screw quadrant (octant)

A metal sextant with special attachments

A set of slates in a case

A log line, reel and log ship

Captain Lewis requested, in this order, the items necessary for "Making a Microscope and fixing Do. on the Index of the Sextant". This was not a microscope as it is today. It consisted of an additional lens and the attachment necessary for mounting it on the sextant. Captain Lewis used it to give the observer a clearer and more defined view of the horizon. The cost of the above order came to one hundred sixty two dollars and twenty cents.
– *Letters of the Lewis and Clark Expedition, Edited by Donald Jackson.*

After acquiring the necessary equipment and training essential to celestial observation, Captain Lewis was instructed in a letter from President Jefferson to use the instruments *"for ascertaining by celestial observations the geography for the country thro' which you will pass."* Beginning at the mouth of the Missouri River, the captains were to plot the course of the Missouri and to fix the location of important places. This included geographic landmarks such as the mouths of major river confluences, islands, rapids and any other landmarks easily recognized.

To plot the course of the Missouri they had to define courses traveled. For this task, Captain Lewis ordered the compasses and a log-line. Using compass bearings and distances from one point to another along a specific bearing, they were able to plot the river's course. This data along with the celestial readings would give Captain Clark the necessary information needed to draft accurate maps of the routes.

While Captain Clark had not been with Captain Lewis as he gathered information and supplies for the expedition, he was at Wood's Camp near St. Louis for several months prior to May 14, 1804, the day the Corps of Discovery set out on their westward journey. During this time Captain Lewis taught him how to use the equipment and record essential data. Captain Clark, the expedition cartographer, was assigned the task of recording all navigational information. He sketched maps and made field notes which he later entered in his journals, describing the courses of the rivers and their water sheds. His logs are the only information of this kind known to exist from Wood's Camp to Fort Mandan.

On July 22, 1804, Captain Lewis described the instruments and processes he and Captain Clark used for celestial observation. At another time, he mentioned taking backward observations when the sun was too high in the sky to use the sextant effectively. If Captain Lewis recorded celestial and course information in his journals for this part of the journey, it has not been found. Of course, the lower Missouri had previously been explored by fur trappers and traders and a lot of information existed about the Missouri River and the surrounding territory up to the Mandan Village. In the spring of 1805 on parting Fort Mandan and heading west, both captains logged data for the remainder of the trip.

The chronometer Captain Lewis purchased in Philadelphia, was calibrated and set on Greenwich Mean Time. The captain found it lost fifteen and one half minutes every twenty four hours. The clock had to be wound and a time adjustment made daily to keep it accurate. It served its purpose well until it stopped or they forgot to wind it. Once that happened it was no better than a good watch for scientific information. They reset it but the estimated 'mean' time was based on local time determined by the position of the sun at high noon rather than Greenwich Mean Time. Why was Greenwich Mean Time important? It was the primary reference for all computations on the astronomical tables and charts.

Although the captains took along some to the latest scientific instruments for fixing locations, they relied heavily on dead reckoning. By carefully determining direction and distances of courses from a predetermined location (St. Louis), they were able to plot their course across the Louisiana Territory, to the Pacific Coast and back again.

Determining latitude was relatively easy but longitude was much more difficult. Latitude is the measurement in degrees, minutes and seconds of a given point north or south of the equator. The equator is at 0° latitude while the North Pole is at 90° latitude. Imagery lines made up of points equal distance from the equator are called parallels or lines of latitude. In the northern hemisphere, the parallels or lines of latitude run east and west but are read south to north. If a reading is 45°N latitude, that simply means it is located somewhere along the 45th parallel, half way between the equator and the North Pole. If the readings is 46°N 48' 26"N as was Captain Lewis' reading for the Travelers' Rest campsite, the point is 11' 34" short of the 47th parallel north. Each degree is divided into sixty minutes (60') and each minute into sixty seconds (60"). A degree of latitiude is equal to approximately sixty nine and two fifths miles or one hundred eleven kilometers. The accurate reading for Travelers' Rest campsite is 46° 45'N.

Lewis' error for this point was long by 3' 26" or approximately three and one half miles.

A point of longitude is the distance in degrees, minutes and seconds of any place east or west of the Prime Meridian (O° Meridian). Lines of longitude or meridians run north and south but are read east to west. Because these lines extend from the north to the south pole they are not equal distance from each other. The widest point between lines of longitude is at the equator and from there they merge meeting at the poles. A degree of longitude varies in distance as the location of the point moves north or south of the equator. For instance, a degree of longitude at the equator is equal to approximately sixty nine miles while a degree of longitude at the 45th parallel is approximately forty nine miles. A longitudinal reading is determined by the relationship between distance and time as the sun passes from east to west. The earth rotates fifteen degrees easterly every hour, totaling three hundred sixty degrees in twenty four hours. Captain Lewis compared the local time when the sun was at its highest point in the sky (noon) with the time the sun was in the same position at the Prime or 0° Meridian. The difference in these times (hours, minutes and seconds) could then be changed to the distance west of the Prime Meridian in degrees, minutes and seconds. So having Greenwich Mean Time was important for accurate calculations. To take celestial observations for determining longitude, several men were required. They made a number (Captain Lewis often used seven or eight) of observations of several celestial bodies in rapid secession. The readings had to be timed and carried out according to a specific plan. Many variances were taken into consideration in the astronomical tables, such as the earth's orbit and the bending of light as it passes through the earth's atmosphere. In addition to these calculated factors, there were others affecting accuracy for which there were no corrections in the tables: 1. Once the chronometer ran down or stopped, its was no longer dependable for Greenwich Mean Time; 2. Conditions in the field varied greatly from place to place due to geography and/or weather; 3. The wooden arms of the octant was subject to warping due to changes in barometric conditions and humidity; 4. On the journey, there was little time to perform the difficult tasks; 5. The men were often exhausted; 6. Computations required far too much time for the captains to complete in the field; 7. And, of course, there was the factor of human error. In spite of the difficulties, the captains made the observations as directed by the president.

On the Corps return in September of 1806, following a brief stay in St.

Louis, Captain Lewis traveled to Washington to meet with President Jefferson. After a quick debriefing, the president directed Captain Lewis to give Ferdinand Rudolph Hassler, a West Point professor of mathematics, the celestial readings. Mr. Hassler was to complete the mathematical calculations and make the necessary corrections to plot the exact courses of the Corps of Discovery. After several attempts, Mr. Hassler gave up. He claimed he was unable to make the calculations from the data presented and that he had been given only one of the journals which, in his opinion, was poorly written. Given Hassler's report, President Jefferson considered much of the celestial data to be irrelevant and basically useless.

Possibly disappointed by the fact that there was no easy passage to the Pacific, the president made few arrangements to preserve the information, specimens or equipment of the expedition. With the exception of what he kept or sent to museums, most of the collections were lost. The captains and other members of the expedition must have been disappointed to see their hard work disregarded as having little or no value. Each expedition journalist was allowed to keep his journals. It is only by the value each journalist and other interested persons placed on their work that a recorded history of the expedition exists today. Shortly after the Corps of Discovery's return, the scientific instruments along with other valuable items used in the expedition were auctioned off in St. Louis for very little money.

For almost two hundreds years, Captains Lewis and Clark's celestial data was assumed useless by most Lewis and Clark enthusiasts. Thanks to the work of Dr. Robert Bergantino, Montana Tech, University of Montana, at Butte, Montana, that assumption has been disproved. He and other scientists have made the difficult mathematical calculations and determined that the celestial observations of the expedition were indeed significant. They found the readings to be surprisingly accurate – given the lack of adequate training and the circumstances under which the data was collected. As with all the scientific information recorded in the journals, Captains Lewis and Clark's careful descriptions and remarkable detail in fixing points of longitude and latitude can no longer go unnoticed or unappreciated.

THE SWEAT LODGE

Along the trail on September 12, 1805, Clark *"saw near an old Indian encampment a Swet house Covered with earth"*. *(Thwaites 3, p.62)*
No early-day Indian camp was complete without a sweat lodge. The

vast majority of Indians in North America used the sweat lodge in one form or another. The nearest thing to it in the white man's world is the Finnish sauna.

Religious significance is interlaced with the lodge preparations and its actual use. The type of framework erected was universal among the plains tribes except for very minor variations. For the average frame, twelve to fourteen willow shoots, eight to ten feet long, were set upright in the ground to form a circle about seven feet across. The sticks for the doorway, which always faced the east, would be set first, two feet apart. Holes six to eight inches deep were made in the ground with an iron or wooden pin, and the butts of the willows were set in these holes. Opposite the doorway, on the west side, two more willow were placed. After marking the center of the lodge with a peg, one used a cord to measure the distance to each willow. The remaining willows were set in pairs to complete the circle, each shoot opposite another.

When all the willows had been placed, each doorway shoot was bent toward the center and its opposing shoot at the west bent to meet it; the two were twisted together at a height of about four feet. The remaining shoots, making the north and south sides of the lodge, were then bent across the east-west arches and twisted together, in the same way, forming a dome-shaped hut.

The floor of the sweat lodge was covered with sage and the framework covered with hides (later years, canvas and old quilts), to keep it dark inside. The average lodge would accommodate four to six people. A pit was dug in the center measuring about fifteen inches in diameter and twelve inches deep, and the earth taken from it was carefully piled in a mound about six feet from the door. This mound represented the earth on which we live; some of the dirt was spread to the door to make a path – the Good Road. Eight or ten feet east of the mound a large fire was laid for heating stones. The stones were gathered from a hillside, not a riverbed, and selected to stand heat without splitting or crumbling. Stone of volcanic variety is considered better than granite or quartz that crumble or explode when heated and doused with water. About twelve stones, each the size of two fists, were chosen. The fire was laid by placing four pieces of firewood, about three feet long and a few inches thick, parallel to the ground pointing east and west. After kindling was added, and four more pieces of wood facing north-south, and then more kindling, the rocks were set on top. The fire was lit from the east side, and in less than an hour the heated rocks would become almost white-hot.

Although the process of participating in the sweat bath may vary somewhat from one Indian Nation to another, the following description is one way. Participants, naked except for breechclouts, file into the lodge in a clockwise direction. The leader, or medicine man, is the last to enter. All sit down cross-legged. After a purifying ceremony, an assistant standing outside uses two stout wooden forks to bring the hot rocks to the fire pit in the center of the sweat lodge. Placement of the rocks is done in a prescribed and significant manner. The leader passes around a bucket of water and each member wets himself down. The door is finally closed from the outside, and in the darkness, the leader splashes water onto the stones. Soon stifling hot steam fills the lodge. The intense heat makes one sweat profusely. When the limit of endurance as been reached, the leader instructs the assistant to open the door. Cool fresh air is welcomed. Then the door is once more closed and more water is splashed on the hot rocks. One feels nearly physically and mentally cooked, when the door is again opened. There are yet two more sessions, and when the door covering is lifted the last time, all file out – moving around the lodge to the left. They wash with cold water to remove the sweat and dirt, or jump in a nearby stream.

Sweathouse baths offered both spiritual and physical cleansing and strengthening. It was traditional to sing medicine songs during the bath. Nez Perce women went to the lodge for purification after their menstrual periods ended and before and after childbirth. Following the death of a family member, a sweat bath was essential for the spiritual cleansing and purification of either men or women after handling the body of the deceased. Temporary Nez Perce sweat lodges were covered with hides, but the more permanent ones were layered with grass, sod, and more grass. Both women and men used the lodges separately, and if there was only one house, the men always used it first. Sweat baths were to purify internally as well as externally, spiritually as well as physically.

HORSES FOR THE CORPS

Many elements decided the success of the Lewis and Clark Expedition: leadership, preparation, ingenuity, fortitude, luck, Sacajawea's presence, help from the tribes met along the way, and very importantly, their horses. Although some of the horses were found, rented, or received as gifts, most were obtained through trade with the Indians. Bartering for them with such items as beads, clothing, firearms and kettles, they paid from $20.00 to $120.00 in today's currency.

It is often unclear how many horses accompanied the Expedition at any one time. During the first winter encampment at Camp Dubois, an unknown number of horses were used for hunting and hauling supplies. Some accompanied the party as they journeyed up the Missouri to the Mandan Villages. At St. Charles, Missouri, the explorers began with four horses. George Drouillard and one or more designated riders used these when hunting. The Expedition had no stock while traveling from the Mandans until reaching the Continental Divide.

With great joy and relief the explorers finally met the Shoshone Indians and arranged to purchase some of their horses, without which the passage over the Rocky Mountains would have been next to impossible. The horses they acquired from the Shoshone were mostly castoffs, as a number of them appeared to be sore-backed, not accustomed to packs, in poor condition, and young. On August 24th Lewis purchased three horses and a mule. For the horses he gave an axe, a knife, a handkerchief and a pair of leggings. The mule, a cross between a horse and a donkey, was a rare animal in this part of the country and commanded twice the cost of a horse. Lewis considered the mule a "great acquisition". He also gave Charbonneau some

Horses played a vital role in the capability of the Corps of Discovery to transport themselves and their gear over rugged, mountainous terrain. Photo courtesy Patricia Hastings.

items with which to buy Sacajawea a horse. Four days later he purchased twenty-two more horses, and with a few additional animals bought with items such as a pistol, 100 balls, powder, a knife, and a musket, the party started over the Bitterroot Mountains with approximately forty horses.

On September 2nd Clark wrote of the treacherous mountainous journey. *"Several horses fell Some turned over, and others Sliped down Steep hill Sides, one horse Crippeled & 2 gave out."* (Thwaites 3, p.50) Many of their horses sustained injuries. However, when the Corps met the Salish Indians at present-day Ross's Hole, the Captains were able to exchange seven of the poorer horses for eleven of the Salish horses; Clark considered these "elegant horses". "The exchange may well have made the difference, for lesser horses probably could not have survived the extreme weather and hazards that followed." (Gibbons, p.27)

Upon arriving at Travelers' Rest with approximately forty-five horses and one mule, the animals were awarded a full day of rest before continuing on. The following nine days would prove nearly impossible for the explorers but for the packhorses. During the harrowing crossing of the mountainous Lolo Pass, hunger drove the party to eat five horses; other animals were lost or abandoned when too badly injured.

When the Corps finally met the Nez Perce Nation on the Weippe Prairie, the number of stock was thirty-eight. Within two weeks the Expedition made dugout canoes for continuing the journey by water. Not needing the animals until their return, they were left in the care of Chief Twisted Hair and his two sons. The thirty-seven horses and one mule were branded for future identification. Whitehouse described the branding in his journal. They *"cropped their fore mane, and branded them with a Sturrup Iron on the near fore Shoulder, So that we may know them again at our return."* *(Moulton 11, p.338)* If Lewis did not have an actual tack stirrup in his supplies, Shields, the blacksmith could have fashioned an oval stirrup for this purpose. (In later western history, cowboys commonly used the circle shape in various combinations for branding.)

The following spring the Expedition acquired twenty-three horses from Indians on the upper Columbia before reaching the Nez Perce, and upon finally retrieving their branded stock Twisted Hair was holding for them, only two were missing. Old Toby, the Corps' Shoshone guide had taken both when he abandoned the party the previous October. Other animals were bought from or given as gifts by the Nez Perce. During the next several weeks, other animals were acquired, given, lost or eaten. On May 5th Clark was given a gray mare in thanks for treating the eyes of a Nez Perce man.

During the spring the horses were so restless that even when hobbled or picketed during the night, some escaped. By May 14th Lewis found the stallions so troublesome that he tried to exchange them for mares or geldings; even though he offered two for one, the Nez Perce were uninterested. With no alternative, the captains resolved to castrate the animals. *"One of the Indians present offered his services on this occasion he cut them without tying the string of the stone as is usual, and assures us that they will do much better in that way."* (Thwaites 5 p.35) Drouillard also helped by gelding two of the stallions *"in the usual way"*. Here was an opportunity for Lewis to judge which method was preferable.

By the next day all were swollen but appeared to be doing better than the two Drouillard had cut, and within a week he declared that those cut by the Indians were recovering faster, did not suffer, or swell as much as those *"cut in the common way"*. Nevertheless, Lewis' horse fell victim to the operation. The animal's condition was failing and he was in great pain. As there was no hope of recovery, his horse was shot on June 1st.

When the party returned to Travelers' Rest, the animal inventory on July 1st was listed at sixty-seven. Lewis reported, *"our horses have stood the journey supprisingly well, most of them are yet in fine order and only want a few days rest to restore them perfectly."* (Thwaites 5, p.175) Two days later the Captains split the Expedition. Lewis took nine men and seventeen horses for traveling north, and the remaining party, including forty-nine horses and the mule, went south with Clark. Because of a subsequent skirmish on the Upper Marias River, Lewis, fearing pursuit by the Blackfeet, abandoned the horses at his disposal and fled via the white pirogue and five small canoes down the Missouri River.

In the meantime, Clark headed south with his beasts of burden laden with supplies, his men, and Sacajawea with her son, Pomp, now nearly eighteen months old. When they reached the Yellowstone River, the men busied themselves cutting trees and dressing skins for building watercraft. With great dismay they awoke the morning of July 21st to discover some Indians had stolen twenty-four of the horses. On the 24th, as Clark and most of the party put on the river, Sergeant Pryor and three privates were dispatched to drive the remaining horses overland to the Mandan Villages. But two nights later thieves also took the remaining animals. Pryor and his men were left to continue on foot. Upon reaching "Pompys Tower" they made bullboats with buffalo hides and floated down the Yellowstone River to miraculously intercept the rest of the Expedition on August 8th.

Historic ponderosa pine situated near Colt Killed Creek north of the Powell Ranger Station in Idaho that was peeled by Native Americans long ago for its inner bark and cambium layer. Some historians believe this tree to be one that some members of the Expedition actually saw and commented on in the journals. Photo courtesy Patricia Hastings.

CULTURALLY PEELED TREES

The practice of harvesting the inner bark and cambium layers of trees for nutritional, medicinal and industrial uses by the indigenous peoples of the Inland Pacific Northwest has been long established. Today, evidence of this use is found on the culturally scarred trees that have escaped timber harvesting or natural destruction such as fire or disease. They stand as living artifacts of former human subsistence patterns.

Specimens of these trees remain in scattered clusters and as single trees along the Lolo Trail system. Within this geographic area four species have been recorded for their culturally peeled bark. They are the ponderosa pine, lodgepole pine, western red cedar and whitebark pine.

The use of ponderosa pine as a food source was first described in Clark's journal at the encampment on September 12, 1805, *"I mad camp on this roade & particularly on this Creek the Indians have peeled a number of Pine for the under bark which they eate at certain Seasons of the year, I am told in the Spring they make use of this bark."* (Thwaites 3,p.63)

In the spring when the sap was running, the women traditionally peeled long, narrow strips of bark from the ponderosa tree trunk. The inner bark or cambium layer was scraped from the outer bark and eaten raw as a sweet and chewy delicacy. It was also made into cakes and stored for future use. The peeled cambium from lodgepole pine was used for human consumption like the ponderosa cambium, but more likely, along the Lolo Trail, it was shredded and used fresh or dried as feed for horses when grass was in short supply. The bark of the western red cedar was peeled in rectangular strips for basket making. (Merrell 1998 p.2-5)

The peeled trees are indicators of travel corridors, meeting places and resting spots. We know from history that both the Nez Perce and Salish Indians frequented this land bridge, the Lolo Trail, between the plains on the eastern side of the Rocky Mountains and the Columbia Plateau region westward. At the "Indian Post Office" site along this Trail, there are over two hundred peeled lodgepole trees.

A three-hundred-year-old dead ponderosa still stands in a forested area near Colt Killed Creek, (also known as White Sand Creek). This tree exhibits the classic peeled scar and is considered a "Historical Ponderosa Pine" by the U.S. Forest Service. It is located on the route taken by the Corps on their westward journey when Old Toby, their guide, erroneously followed a fishing trail down to the Lochsa River. (See photo) The nature of the cambium scar on this ponderosa is impressive for its size and classic rectangular shape.

It is not unusual for scars to exceed two to three feet in width and extend over five feet in height. Considering the distinctive size, it is not surprising that Clark used them as trail guides in the snowstorm on June 17, 1806. The party was near the Lolo Trail on Hungry Creek making their first attempt to cross the Bitterroot Mountains on their return trip. In Clark's words, *"This mountain we ascended about 3 miles when we found ourselves invelloped in snow from 8 to 12 feet deep even on the south side of the mountain. I was in front and could only prosue the derection of the road by the trees which had been peeled by the natives for the inner bark of which they Scraped and eate, as those peeled trees were only to be found Scattered promisquisley, I with great difficulty prosued the direction of the road one mile further to the top of the mountain."* (Thwaites 5,p.142)

Unfortunately, only a relatively few of these peeled trees remain along the Lolo Trail today. The ponderosa was in high demand for the timber industry; forest fires also caused the destruction of many mature trees.

The second most popular tree is the lodgepole. Not only is the bark thinner than the ponderosa making it easier to peel, its high nutritional value made it an excellent food source for both man and horse.

Scarred lodgepole pines have survived in the highest numbers along the length of the Lolo Trail. There are several reasons that may explain this dominance of the lodgepole among other species used for cultural peeling. One is that the ponderosa do not thrive along windy ridge tops. Early logging and forest fires, both natural and man made, left the terrain open to the lodgepole pine forests that grow quickly in a regenerating forest ecosystem. (Merrell, 2001, p.29)

On September 11, 1805, Joseph Whitehouse described in his journal another instance of a culturally altered tree. He *"passed a tree on which was a number of Shapes drawn on it with paint by the natives. A white bear Skin hung on the Same tree. We Suppose this to be a place of worship among them."* (Thwaites 7,p154) His observation was made as the party was approaching today's Woodman's Creek, the first campsite after leaving Travelers' Rest.

In 1999, because of the upcoming Lewis and Clark Bicentennial, the United States Forest Service initiated a systematic inventory of heritage and cultural values for Lolo Pass, an area rich with evidence of American Indian history and turn-of-the-century mining and trapping. Utilizing work-studies such as the Passport in Time (PIT) "Written in the Trees" project, the Forest Service has been actively recording many of the existing peeled trees in that region.

One such study was held in the summer of 2000 under the direction of Jeff Fee, archeologist from the Kooskia Ranger Station, Kooskia, Idaho, and assisted by Carolynne Merrell, contract archeologist. As a volunteer participant, this writer helped in the recording effort within an extended grove of lodgepole pine trees. Each tree was given a number, then a detailed inventory was taken of each tree's location, noting whether it was dead or alive, tree species, number of scars, diameter, scar width and length, distance of scar from the ground, and compass direction of the scar.

A pencil sketch and photograph completed the process, unless a core boring was also done to determine the tree's age and the date when the bark was stripped. Dendorchronology – the study of annual tree rings to determine past events – on a number of trees indicated the bark was stripped in various years from 1788 into the early 1900's. Trees were probably peeled long before this date, but they have not survived.

An occasional tree exhibited more than one modification. Deep chunks removed with a hatchet are called "pitch blazes". Hunters and trappers had discovered that chips of wood from old peeled scars made excellent fire starting material. A few trees had a horizontal "V" wedge cut into them. This is a "martin set", used in arranging a jig for trapping pine martins. An "arbor-glyph" is the term given to carved letters or numbers on the scar. Records of these culturally peeled trees and the subsequent modifications are helping to preserve our knowledge of this arterial route used for centuries by Native Americans and subsequent pioneers.

ARMY "REGS"

The majority of the men recruited for the Lewis and Clark Expedition were volunteers from the United States Army. Nearly all the other volunteers hailed from Kentucky, Indiana, Illinois and Missouri and were enlisted as soldiers. Regardless of how they joined the Expedition, all members, including interpreters, were subject to military law and discipline. A large part of the Corps' identification as a military unit was embedded in the clothing they wore and their overall uniformity.

The Captains' and other surviving journals give clues as to the military nature of the voyage and how normal military procedures continued in the "wilderness". One reads about soldiers standing formal guard duty in various camps and in the three forts built during the voyage. The leaders conducted frequent formal inspections of the men's clothing, arms and

An excavation unit being carefully worked at the latrine site at the Travelers' Rest encampment. This exercise proved to be of immeasurable value. Photo courtesy Loren Flynn.

accessories. Courts-martial were held to discipline those who violated the rules of the Articles of War; those convicted were punished. At imposing ceremonies the officers and soldiers dressed in formal uniforms to awe and impress Native peoples.

When an Army unit was on the move, it lived in canvas shelters. Encampments of tents were regulated by Baron Frederick Wilhelm von Steuben's *Regulations for the Order and Discipline of the Troops of the United States,* originally written in 1778 and republished in 1794. The Army called it the "Blue Book". The prescribed camp layout was given in great detail, including drawings of tent placement and arrangement of the cooking fire pits and wagons; and privies or "sinks" were measured at a distance of three hundred feet from the camp. (After archeologists located the Corps' Travelers' Rest fire pit and the latrine in 2002, the distance between them was found to measure the regulation 300 feet.) Necessity dictated the camp cookfire and gunsmith area to be located near a source of water. In 2002 archeologists located the Corps' Travelers' Rest central cookfire next to a now dry side channel of Lolo Creek. This passageway very well may have held water during the Expedition's stay. It is here excavations revealed fire-cracked rock, charcoal, a musket ball and a puddle of lead, indicators of a large fire with intense heat. Native American campfires are less intense in heat than those used for gunsmithing, and the tribes in this surrounding area did not have the technology to melt lead and make musket balls. These facts pointed to this fire pit as belonging to the Corps of Discovery, and may be where Private John Shields repaired some of their guns on July 1-2, 1806.

From the start, the explorers erected tent camps reflecting the Blue Book guidelines, but surely were appropriate to their unique situation. Nevertheless, such regulations changed by the time the party reached the Pacific Coast because their tents had fallen into shreds. On November 28th Clark wrote, *"we are all wet bedding and Stores, having nothing to keep our Selves or Stores dry, our Lodge [Charbonneau's tipi] nearly worn out, and the pieces of Sales & tents So full of holes & rotten that they will not keep anything dry." (Thwaites 3, p.254)*

The following spring, when back in Nez Perce country, they resorted to making tents of sticks and grass. On May 14th, Lewis strengthened his fortification with *"pine poles and brush and the party formed themselves very comfortable tents with willow poles and grass . . . these were made perfectly secure as well from heat of the sun as from rain. We had a bower constructed for ourselves under which we set by day and sleep under the part of an old sail now our only tent as the leather lodge has become rotten and unfit for use."*

Archeologist Dan Hall holds some "likely looking" material from the latrine. Photo courtesy Loren Flynn.

Each excavation unit was carefully measured and developed as the investigation developed. Photo courtesy Loren Flynn.

(Thwaites 5, p.39) Even with prescribed military regulations, in an extended assignment such as the Expedition's, tent protocol became compromised when the materials disintegrated. [The "fortification" Lewis referred to was situated in a round depression in the ground measuring thirty feet in diameter and four feet deep. The Nez Perce had previously used this depression where they built a semi-subterranean circular structure for separate sleeping quarters for the unmarried of each sex over fourteen years of age.] (James, p.33)

In 1801 the Army instigated new uniformity regulations, published by the Office of the Purveyor General, which were in effect until 1808. Regulations included an order that forced all officers and men to cut their hair short and be clean-shaven. Men were to shave three times a week and get a haircut once a month. Military protocol and Lewis' enforcement of it suggested these explorers continued to wear their hair short, even during the hardships of the trek across the continent. However, during some of the more demanding portions of the route their hair did become somewhat shaggy. When Lewis finally made contact with the Shoshones he wrote that his hair was *"deshivled"*, indicating this was an unusual circumstance. Even so, on August 19th he stated that the white men blended in with the Indian men, all of whom had cut their hair as a sign of mourning after loss of some of their members to the Minnetares; Cameahwait's hair was *"cut close all over his head"*. *(Thwaites 2, p.372)* On the following day the main chief tied to Clark's hair six small pieces of shells. Surely, his hair was also longer than usual. But when the party could remain in camp long enough to rest, repair clothing, make moccasins and hunt for food, they would bring their appearance back into conformity. No mention was ever made of running out of soap or razors. Thus, while the Corps rested along "Travellers Creek" in September 1805, it is very likely that the men took time to adhere to the established regulations.

SAVING THE GLADE CREEK CAMPSITE

The Lewis and Clark campsite at Glade Creek atop Lolo Pass was recently rescued from an impending logging operation. This was because of the quick action of Carolynne Merrell, a contract archeologist. Early in September 1997, she was inventorying peeled trees in that area and was alarmed to find that a timber company was about to begin logging in the glade. Trees in the heart of the campsite were marked with paint, and bulldozers had begun opening logging access roads. With great urgency, Merrell called James R. Fazio, past president of the Idaho Chapter of the Lewis and Clark Trail Heritage Foundation, who immediately initiated a quickly moving crusade.

His first call was to Denny Sigars, the industrial forester for that area, a man with whom Fazio had worked in the past. Prior to this, they had explored one proposal, the possibility of trading the Glade Creek parcel to the Forest Service in return for timberland elsewhere having less historic value. But, as Sigars explained, after years of fruitless negotiating with the Forest Service, the logging company had lost patience and had decided to wait no longer in taking the timber from Glade Creek.

This knowledge prompted Fazio to communicate via e-mail with every powerful and interested person he thought might be interested in the issue, including the press, local TV, state government officials, and the executive director of the Idaho State Historical Society. Also, by a stroke of luck, on the following day (September 10th), historian Stephen Ambrose was to be the featured speaker at a fund-raiser benefitting the Idaho Humanities Council. A few state legislators and lobbyists planning to attend were friendly to the cause of history and conservation. Best of all, when Ambrose

Clearwater National Forest sign at the Glade Creek Campsite in Idaho. Photo courtesy Patricia Hastings.

heard about the Glade Creek news, he was most distressed; surely he would be a helpful ambassador.

Within a few days, activities stimulated by Fazio's outreach resulted in a meeting at the Glade Creek site; all those concerned attended. After lengthy discussion, representatives from the timber company agreed to halt the logging and wait one more year in hopes someone would buy the land. With another stroke of good fortune, it became known that the Idaho Heritage Trust was looking to support a worthy cause, possibly something related to Lewis and Clark. Thus, Heritage Trust funds, along with generous donations from the Idaho Power Company and others, raised $225,770.00 to purchase the 160 acres of the glade and the surrounding forest. "Ownership of the site was then transferred to the Idaho Department of Parks and Recreation for management in a natural state with minimum intrusion of access paths and interpretive signs," (Fazio, p.65)

MISSOULA

"Is-u-la," is a cry of surprise and horror uttered by the Salish Indians when they encountered their enemies, the Blackfeet, waiting to ambush and kill them in the Clark Fork River Canyon. Early French traders called the canyon "La Porte de Infer" translated, "gate of hell," consequently the names "Missoula" and "Hellgate" for the city and the canyon.

Missoula's first structure, a two-room cabin built by William Hamilton near Rattlesnake Creek, did not become the trading post envisioned by Mr. Hamilton, who only succeeded in selling whiskey. In 1859-60 Lieutenant John Mullan was directing the construction of a military road, commonly called "the Mullan Road" from Walla Walla, Washington, to Fort Benton, Montana. The route followed an Indian trail along the bank of the Clark Fork River along present day Front Street in Missoula.

Three enterprising men, Francis Worden, Christopher Higgins, who had worked on the Mullan Road, and their clerk, Frank Woody, arrived from Walla Walla in 1860 with a pack train of merchandise and permission to trade with the Flathead Indians. These early entrepreneurs, now recognized as the founders of Missoula, established a trading post, Hell Gate Ronde, on the Mullan Road near the confluence of the Bitterroot and Clark Fork Rivers.

Soon twenty-nine former Mullan Road crew members, attracted to the valley, joined other settlers in petitioning for a new county, to be called

"Bitterroot." The Washington Territorial Legislature ignored "Bitterroot" and created Missoula County. Four years later Worden and Higgins, joined by David Pattee, built a sawmill and flour mill near Rattlesnake Creek, and named them The Missoula Mills Company. They then moved their Hell Gate post to the mill site, which eventually became the city of Missoula

Like similar western frontier towns, Missoula endured bank robberies, an influx of gold miners, gamblers, prostitutes, shootings, and violence. In 1864, Vigilantes from Virginia City, Montana, followed members of the infamous Henry Plummer gang of highwaymen to Hell Gate where they proceeded to try and hang them at Higgins' and Worden's post. Fort Missoula was built in 1877 in response to apprehensive citizens concerned about Indian wars which never did occur in western Montana.

Gradually, a law-abiding settlement, known as "The Garden City," developed at the hub of five western valleys, Missoula, Flathead, Bitterroot, Blackfoot and Hellgate. Agriculture and timber became leading industries. In 1895, the Missoula delegates to the legislature succeeded, with some political tradeoffs, in obtaining the University of Montana for Missoula which has become the definition of the city's character, "progressive and liberal." The Forestry School at the University, The Regional Center of the U.S. Forest Service and the Smoke Jumpers Center are located here. Missoula entered the twenty-first century boasting a strong economic climate and commercial hub, and a regional medical center. The U.S. Census in 2000 positioned Missoula, with a population of 57,053, to challenge Great Falls as Montana's second largest city. However, rapid growth has also brought problems; traffic congestion, urban sprawl, big box stores and homogenous malls. Meanwhile, Missoula manages to attract commerce and tourists while still preserving its vital downtown area, and maintaining its identity as a university town.

BONNER AND MILLTOWN

Two adjacent communities, Bonner and Milltown, just to the east of Missoula, grew around two sawmills which form an intriguing sidelight in the feud between Butte's copper kings, Marcus Daly and W.A. Clark.

In 1882, lumber interests from Missoula including E .L. Bonner and joined by Marcus Daly purchased land for a sawmill allegedly for $100 and a cow. The mill, Blackfoot Milling and Manufacturing Incorporation, was built in 1886. The Northern Pacific Railroad became the largest owner of

*The wooden sculpture
in Bonner, Montana,
depicting Captain Meriwether
Lewis and his dog, Seaman.
Photo courtesy Patricia Hastings.*

forest land in Montana, holding 14,000,000 acres in government land grants. The lumber interests gained control of timber rights through the Northern Pacific Railroad and supplied lumber for the railroads and for the mines of Butte and smelters in Anaconda and Great Falls. The town which developed around the saw mill is named "Bonner" for Missoula entrepreneur, E. L. Bonner. Neat little bungalows comprise the company town. A company store once sold provisions to the mill employees on credit and then deducted from their paychecks.

In 1898, Daly's Anaconda Mining Company acquired the sawmill along with vast tracts of lumber. Daly died in 1900 but his Anaconda company continued. W.A. Clark, Daly's copper king rival, assembled a sawmill, the Western Lumber Company, at Milltown in 1910. In 1919, fires destroyed the Bonner mill, but it was rebuilt in less than a year. Following Clark's death in 1920 Anaconda purchased the mill at Milltown in 1928 and phased it out in 1931-1932.

The Anaconda Company no longer exists. The mill at Bonner is now the property of Stimson Lumber Company, a West Coast based group. On July 4, 1806, Captain Lewis and his men traveled through the area of present-day Bonner. The town, in early 2003, erected a kiosk and a chainsaw wooden sculpture by Ovando artist Jim Rogers, depicting Captain Meriwether Lewis and his dog, Seaman.

The Lolo Pass Visitor Center in 2002. Photo courtesy Bodell Construction Co.

LOLO PASS VISITOR CENTER

Lolo Pass has always been a destination and a meeting place. We have seen how this area is rich in past history; now more recently, folks come in the summer to hike, bike, retrace the trail of the Lewis and Clark Expedition, and to enjoy the camas blooming at Packer Meadows. In the fall they hunt deer and elk, and in the winter the area is a favorite recreation spot for snowmobiles and cross-country skiers.

Lolo Pass straddles the Montana – Idaho border on U.S. Highway 12 and is the dividing line between the Clearwater National Forest on the Idaho side and the Lolo National Forest in Montana. The Clearwater Forest's Powell, Idaho, District administers the pass. In 1979 they moved the old Mud Creek Cabin that had sat for years across from Lolo Hot Springs, to the Pass to serve as a visitor center. Detached were a small winter warming hut and an outhouse.

After more than a decade of ever growing winter use, there was no question about needing a better facility including a telephone and restrooms. Also, the increased tourism engendered by the upcoming Bicentennial of the Lewis and Clark Expedition promised further impact on summertime use.

Eight years ago plans began for constructing a building with updated conveniences, more space for interpretive displays, and enlarged parking areas. Idaho Gov. Dirk Kempthorne took interest in the project while he was still a congressional representative and was instrumental in attaining highway money for the project. Funding for the four and a half million dollar facility came from the United States Forest Service, the federal Transportation Enhancement Act, the Idaho Transportation Department, and the Montana Department of Transportation.

The 2,400 square foot visitor center was completed late in the fall of 2002 with the Opening Day festivities held on December 13th. Built by Bodell Construction of Missoula, Montana, using massive Lodgepole logs measuring ten to fourteen inches in diameter, the structure contains an office, interpretive displays, books and maps for sale, a video room, and chairs for lounging before the fireplace while enjoying a hot drink.

Lolo Pass is now an official year-round rest area for both states, complete with modern restrooms, public telephones, generous parking, and even an area for semi trucks. For seasonal use, a half-mile loop nature trail has been created for those interested in the plants, animals and the history of the Bitterroot Mountains.

The Forest Service, in cooperation with the Nez Perce and Salish-Kootenai tribes, is planning a new interpretive display by the summer of 2003. "Lolo Pass as a crossroads" will be the theme of the exhibit.

THE LOLO MOTORWAY

Constructed by the Civilian Conservation Corps in the 1930s, the Lolo Motorway, U. S. Forest Service Road 500, is a narrow, one lane, unimproved road extending west from Powell Junction to Canyon Junction, Idaho. This seventy-three-mile route follows in close proximity the old Nez Perce Trail. The Lolo Motorway passes several historical sites, many of which are sacred to Native Americans. It runs along east to west ridges separating the North Clearwater and Lochsa River canyons.

Primary access to the Motorway is from U. S. Highway 12 and Idaho State Highway 11 via Forest Service roads. This undeveloped area has no accommodations other than a few camping spots. Winding through rugged terrain, progress is slow. A high-centered vehicle, a detailed map, food, water and a wilderness guide are recommended. A permit is required from July 15th to October 1st. For information regarding the permit and travel conditions, would-be-travelers can call the Kooskia Ranger Station at 208-926-4274 or the Kamiah Ranger Station at 208-935-2513.

FORT FIZZLE

In 1855, as an increasing number of white settlers moved to the Northwest, the Washington Territorial Governor, Isaac Stevens, persuaded the Nez Perce Indians to give up some of their tribal hunting lands in Idaho for white settlement. Under the conditions of this treaty they would live on a five thousand square mile reservation and in return, be afforded the protection of the federal government.

This seemed to work well until a prospector discovered gold, in 1876 within the boundaries of the reserve. The news spread like wild fire. Prospectors rushed to the area. Convinced they had rights to the land under the auspices of O'Sullivan's Manifest Destiny – trouble began to brew. Fights broke out between the white settlers and the Indians. For the next several years, following the strike, the government was pressured by fortune seekers wanting access to the gold and rich fertile lands of the Wallowa Valley. Tension mounted as the intruders became more demanding.

Fearing war between whites and the Nez Perce, the government authorities and Nez Perce leaders convened a council. The government proposed reducing the size of the reservation by more than three fourths of its original size. One band of Nez Perce, whose home was within the boundaries of the proposed reserve, agreed to the arrangement and signed the treaty. Three other bands living outside the reservation objected, refused to sign and left the council.

They were immediately labeled the non-treaty Nez Perce. Among this group was Chief Weeamotkin, known to the whites as Old Chief Joseph. He had been present when the Corps of Discovery passed through Weippe Prairie in 1805 and again in 1806 on their way to and from the Pacific coast. His people had been cordial and helpful to the Lewis and Clark party. Fur traders and missionaries enjoyed good relations with the Indians for more than fifty years.

After Old Joseph's death, white settlers poured into the Wallowa Valley and began claiming the land as their own. Young Chief Joseph filed complaints with various government agencies. President Grant granted the Wallowa to the Nez Perce and ordered all white settlers out of the area. The whites refused to leave. Thinking they had the God-given right to take the land, they threatened violence. Pressured by the governor of the Oregon Territory and white settlers, President Grant reversed his decision and opened the Wallowa Valley up to white settlement.

The Nez Perce who prided themselves in the fact they had never killed a white man, were pushed – backs to the wall. They had no choice but to leave or defend their homeland. Trying to avoid war, Chief Joseph and other tribal leaders went back to the negotiating table. After some painful and humiliating treatment to a highly respected Nez Perce leader, the unbending government representatives dealt a harsh blow. The non-treaty bands were to be on the reservation by April 1, 1877, or they would be put there by force.

Realizing the futility of continued negotiations, the Nez Perce chiefs returned to their people with the sad news. Hurt and angry, the non-treaty Indians were ready for battle. They vowed not to give up the land where their ancestors were buried. Through much effort, Chief Joseph and his brother, Ollokot, a highly respected warrior, convinced their people to move to the reservation. Knowing they had little chance of surviving a war against the United States Government, Chief Joseph uttered these persuasive word. "It is better to live in peace than to began a war and lie dead." Finally, the tribal council consented to comply with the governments demands. They hurried to round up their livestock and gather belongs. Animals were scattered and streams were swollen with spring run-off. In desperation, Chief Joseph appealed for more time. They were granted thirty days.

Meanwhile, east of the mountains, area residents received news of General Custer's disastrous defeat at the Little Big Horn and of the troubles brewing in Idaho. Fearing an uprising in their own communities, nervous residents of Missoula and the Bitterroot Valley pressured the government to build a manned military fort in the area. In 1877, Fort Missoula was built just east of the mouth of the Bitterroot River.

In Idaho, the Nez Perce were tying up the loose ends of the move when, while camping just outside the boundaries of the reservation, a young Indian was taunted into revenging the death of his father. He, along with two other young males, went on a three-day rampage, killing nineteen to twenty white settlers. Chief Joseph and his brother, Ollokot, were away at the time butchering cattle on the Clearwater River. They were horrified when they returned.

The camp was in turmoil. Old people were crying and beating their tepees with sticks. Young Indians were gathering their possessions and fleeing. To no avail, Chief Joseph tried to get them to wait until General Howard arrived. He felt the general would not hold the entire group responsible for the sins of a few young Indians. Fearing for their lives, most of the non-treaty Indians fled to White Bird and surrounding canyons.

Chief Joseph, Ollokot and the remaining Nez Perce were faced with the difficult decision of going to the reservation and abandoning their people or joining them at their new White Bird camp. Chief Joseph chose the latter. This meant they would surely fight. Fight, they did! Outsmarting the cavalry on every front, they were victorious. But, they knew this was short lived. With unlimited resources, the cavalry would strike again and again – killing more warriors each time. The government would eventually wear them down.

Three non-treaty chiefs convened on the bank of the Clearwater River where they made a difficult and heart-breaking decision. For the safety of their women and children, they would leave Idaho, cross the mountains and join the Crow Indians in eastern Montana. There, they hoped to find sanctuary and once again live and hunt in peace. This was not to be. On July 16, 1877, under the guidance of Chief Looking Glass, three hundred warriors and four hundred fifty women and children pushed two thousand horses east along the torturous Lolo Trail. With heavy hearts and little time to gather provisions, the Nez Perce traveled the age old road to the buffalo for the last time as a free people.

The trip was a struggle for both the Indians and the cavalry. Humiliated by the Indian victories and in a desperate attempt to save face, General Howard and his forces followed in hot pursuit. The 1st Cavalry struggled, with heavy artillery, on the rugged mountainous trail. General Howard telegraphed Fort Missoula to ask for help and to and inform area residents of the Nez Perce flight. The news spread quickly.

In no time, a group of approximately two hundred volunteers joined a garrison of thirty five men under the direction of Captain Charles Rawn near the mouth of Lolo Creek. The Fort Missoula regiment had been instructed to block or delay the advancing Nez Perce until General Howard and the 1st Cavalry could overtake them. The men of the 7th infantry and the volunteers quickly threw up a fort of logs and dirt. There they waited.

On July 25, the Nez Perce arrived above the fort. Three chiefs: Chief Joseph, Chief Looking Glass and Chief White Bird walked down for a parley. The chiefs told the men gathered of their plans to pass through the valley peacefully. They vowed to pay for supplies and to harm no one. Not eager for battle, the volunteers believed the chiefs. They packed up their supplies and returned to their homes and businesses. The 7th Infantry was left holding the fort.

While the soldiers prepared for the next day and slept, the Nez Perce, in a brilliantly-executed plan, stacked their campfires high with wood so they would burn through the night and sent young braves out to make noise as if they were partying. The night guards saw the fires and heard the noise which lasted well into the evening. They never suspected that seven hundred and fifty Indians and two thousand horses were quietly circumventing their garrison on a hillside trail to the north.

Waking to find the Indians had outsmarted them, Captain Rawn and his troops hurried north to Missoula to find the Nez Perce had gone south to Stevensville where they stopped for supplies. Passing peacefully up the Bitterroot Valley as promised, then along the southern Nee Mee Po Trail to Ross' Hole, they turned east and crossed the Continental Divide at Gibbon's Pass to a campsite on the Big Hole River.

The United States government did not give up. Many battles followed as the Nez Perce fled southeast and then to the north. Finding the Crow Indians aiding the cavalry in a conflict against them, the chiefs knew they had only one chance. They must go to Canada. While camped a few miles south of the Canadian border, the Nez Perce were surrounded just north of the Bear Paw Mountains. After several days of intense fighting, they surrendered. They were taken as prisoners, loaded on a flatboat and then put in box cars to be shipped by train to a reservation in Oklahoma. Many became ill and died. Eventually, the survivors were sent to reservations in Washington and Oregon but were never allowed to return to their homeland. Chief Joseph, brokenhearted, died on the Colville Reservation in Washington State.

Shortly after the Nez Perce passage, the fort on Lolo Creek was called "Fort Fizzle" by area settlers who were sympathetic with the Nez Perce people and their plight. The name has stuck. A marker on U. S. Highway 12, five miles west of Travelers' Rest campsite denotes the fort's approximate location.

A PERSONAL JOURNEY
Jean Clary of The Discovery Writers
Summer 2001

A short time after driving up Parachute Hill near U.S. Highway 12 in the rugged mountains of north-central Idaho, we felt as though we were in another country. The aroma of pine trees, dry grass and flowers was unmistakable in the high country of the Nez Perce Trail, the same trail the Corps of Discovery struggled over to the west of Travelers' Rest on their way to the Nez Perce Country. What a feeling of history. I can almost see the struggling men and horses, feel their sense of fear, hopelessness and exhaustion.

Our journey had started at the Powell Ranger Station where we had lunch and picked up some information. We were told the road was rough, and in places we could easily get high centered. It was rough and narrow, but in the truck, we had no problems at all.

Our first stop was at Cayuse Junction or White Sands. We set up our tents, gathered wood and prepared to spend the night. The first meal was an adventure, as were the others. One night we had a special dessert cooked in a Dutch oven. There were very few amenities. The air was so clean, the stars were out and it was very quiet.

The birds woke us early the next morning, and we diverted from the traditional road to Papoose Saddle and Thirteen Mile Camp. At the saddle near the Post Office cairn, we actually stood on the Nez Perce Trail. It was a spiritual experience for me. We were on the real trail many times, but the time I was most deeply moved was on this saddle. There were lupines, dwarf phlox and everywhere heather bloomed, far different from when the Corps of Discovery traveled this route, then covered by snow. It was thought that the rock cairn was used as a place to exchange messages. An archeologist told

Author Jean Clary (at the right) with Billie Houle at the "Indian Post Office" cairn along the Lolo Trail in Idaho.

us that people constantly change the stones, adding and taking away.

Of the two archeologists we met along the trail, one was with the National Park Service and the other, the U.S. Forest Service. They were generous about sharing their knowledge about the trail, emphasizing that the trail was there long before Lewis & Clark traveled over it. Other information they shared was that it was an important travel route for the Nez Perce and the Salish for hundreds of years. The Nez Perce went east to hunt buffalo and the Salish west for salmon. He told us the Salish and Coeur d'Alene spoke the same language. It was also a valuable trade corridor.

At the Cinque Hole, my companions walked down to another campsite of the Corps of Discovery. It was very wet and must have been full of mosquitoes.

We camped two more nights at sites that Lewis and Clark had used. The third day, we drove to Rocky Ridge where you could see to the North Fork of the Clearwater River. The last night we were at Lowell at the confluence of the Lochsa and the Selway Rivers, which forms the Clearwater River. At this time, we succumbed to civilization and warm showers, and in a small way experienced the relief the weary Corps of Discovery members felt when they reached and bathed in the hot springs of upper Lolo Creek on their return to Travelers' Rest; I wondered how many others who follow in the footsteps of these explorers have shared similar thoughts.

HONORS FOR CAPTAIN CLARK, YORK AND SACAJAWEA

When Captain Meriwether Lewis recruited William Clark to help lead the Corps of Discovery, he promised him the rank of Captain. Clark never got the commission. However, on January 17, 2001, President William J. Clinton conferred the appointment to the rank of Captain in the United States Army to William Clark in honor to his service to his country.

Also President Clinton bestowed the honorary promotion to the rank of Sergeant in the United States Army to Sacagawea "so that all Americans might recognize her critical role in Lewis and Clark's journey to the sea."

"In recognition of York's selfless contributions to the Corps of Discovery and his service to our country" President Clinton granted the honorary promotion to the rank of Sergeant in the United States Army to York, "the slave who accompanied Lewis and Clark to the Pacific and back."

THE OLD DUTCH LADY

Atop a steep hillside overlooking the valley of Travelers' Rest, stands an outcropping of rock that mostly goes unnoticed by passing motorists. A pine tree partially obscures the face of it, and as it is on private property, visitors are rare. A long-time resident of Lolo says the locals refer to the rock formation as "The Old Dutch Lady" because, in a side view it appears as a head of a woman wearing a Dutch cap. He remembers when the Lolo highway was being rebuilt in 1949. Needing more rock for the project, the

The rock known as "The Old Dutch Lady". Photo courtesy Patricia Hastings.

construction engineer was about to blast this nearby stone outcrop. When the local people heard about it, they pleaded to leave her untouched, and were successful in saving her. (The Lolo road became classified as a Secondary road in April of 1947, and as a Forest Highway Project in 1949, road improvements were made and paving begun.)

Bud Moore in his book, *The Lochsa Story* (p. 25-26), describes with delightful sensitivity, this stone-faced woman:

"Nobody knows, nor will anyone ever know when the first pilgrims crossed the mountains via the valley of the Lolo Fork and the Lochsa Country. Whoever he was, his tracks began to wear a trail that, in time, became the Road to the Buffalo for the Ni-me-poo (Nez Perce) and the route to the salmon for the Flathead Indians who lived in the Bitterroot Valley. A stone-faced woman stands on the foothills near where the trail enters the plains of the Bitterroot, facing west toward the mountains.

"Her bust is twenty feet tall; her perfume is sage warmed by the summer sun; her voice the whisper of winds in pines growing close at her side. She rose some 12,000 years ago from the subsiding waters of ancient Lake Missoula to become a visible Native American."

U.S. FOREST SERVICE

Although Travelers' Rest State Park is not part of the Lolo National Forest, national forest land is nearby. Consequently, the U.S. Forest Service, though not responsible for Travelers' Rest, has been involved behind the scenes with other agencies and with the Native American tribes in obtaining and establishing the Travelers' Rest State Park. Since the town of Lolo is unincorporated and has no local government, county, state and federal agencies have worked together to purchase and preserve the site.

The Lolo National Historic Landmark, which includes Travelers' Rest National Historical Landmark, extends from Travelers' Rest west along the Lewis and Clark National Historic Trail. Recently, the U.S. Forest Service negotiated with Plum Creek Timber Company to purchase free title or easement for twenty miles of the trail extending from Howard Creek to Powell, Idaho, thus insuring that this portion of the trail be preserved for future generations. Also, there is an agreement being forged with the Bureau of Land Management, Bitterroot and Lolo National Forests and Fish, Wildlife & Parks, to coordinate Lewis and Clark programs out of Travelers' Rest, according to Margaret Gorski, Lewis and Clark Bicentennial Coordinator for the Forest Service.

At Packers Meadow
June 6, 1938

THE CCC AT PACKER MEADOWS

To put the nation's unemployed young men to work during the Depression years, Congress created the Civilian Conservation Corps (CCC) in April of 1933. President Franklin D. Roosevelt gave the Secretary of War (now Department of Defense) the job of managing the new program.

Guns and bullets would be swapped for picks and shovels to create a type of military operation using WWI leftover supplies, uniforms and equipment. This program was for youth, ages sixteen to twenty-two, some of whom were war veterans and Native Americans. The Army was in charge of subsistence, housing, pay and discipline, while the United States Forest Service administered the work projects. An enrollee earned $30.00 per month, of which $25.00 was vouchered to his family.

The CCC boys were housed in tents and roughly constructed barracks-type camps consisting of a cook house, a commissary, officers quarters with a shower, first aid tent, a system of tents or barracks with showers for the workers, and an outdoor latrine. On the parade ground by the flagpole, the men would stand at attention for mail call.

In the summer of 1933 CCC Camp #F-23, Company #1251, was located at Packer Meadows at Lolo Pass. Wearing military clothes, the young men worked on assignments such as construction on road 500, fire fighting and trail building. CCC Camp #F-47, Company #953 operated there the following summer. Situated on the Selway Forest, this camp was under the Fort Missoula CCC District in Missoula, Montana.

In October of 1934, Packer Meadows became part of the Lolo National

Panorama of a Civilian Conservation Corps (CCC) crew encamped at Packer Meadows in 1935. Photo courtesy K. Ross Toole Archives, University of Montana, Photo No. 74-269.

Forest, but in 1961 it was transferred to the Clearwater National Forest. Records show CCC Camps were also active at Packer Meadows in the summers of 1935 and 1936. (Keating, p. 3)

Over 3.5 million young men were in CCC camps during the period of the program (1933-1942). Working year-round, the summer months were spent in the nation's forests and National Parks in the northern part of the U.S., and the winter months in the southern Forest Service Regions. But the CCC came to an end when the nation's focus turned to WWII, and many of these young men were inducted into the Armed Services. Being involved in the CCC left many of the men with new skills and promising starts in life and later entered rewarding careers, but most importantly had become solid citizens.

LOOKING BACK
A story of a patron at Travelers' Rest, told by Ernie and Pat Deschamps

Native American feet moved often along the old Buffalo Road – today's Lolo Trail. It led them to fields of edible roots, buffalo, celebrations, trade, love, etc. As they moved back and forth through the Bitterroot Valley, and oftentimes across the mountains, the site of Travelers' Rest was often used as a campground. Aerial infrared photographs have found several tepee rings along the area of the site, and it certainly fulfilled requirements for a good campground – water, firewood, and graze for the horses.

On an afternoon in 2000, with a small group touring Travelers' Rest campsite, a Nez Percé woman, eating a piece of red licorice given to her (and to all visitors) took her candy stick and withdrew to a spot beneath a tall pine tree and sat quietly. The old tree overlooked a low-lying plain that lay in the stream bottom north of her, largely untrammeled by the activities of man. She sat still and stared at the unchanged land while eating the red licorice. After a time her companions came to join her and the woman said to them, "I cannot believe any of my heritage is still left and not plowed up, or with houses on it. I can feel the Spirits of my people, they are still here." Before her was the precise location of the ancient Indian campsite that has come to be known, because it was used by The Corps of Discovery on two occasions, in September of 1805 and again in late June and early July of 1806, as Travelers' Rest.

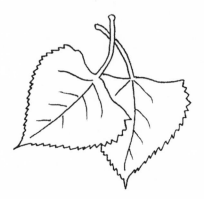

Chapter 10

WHAT'S AHEAD?

The Park is now a reality and exists to preserve this sensitive historical area in perpetuity. Its future depends on the support of those Lewis and Clark enthusiasts, historians, scholars, Native Americans, donors and common people who with the state, federal and local organizations have combined their efforts to make this project possible. Working together, these organizations have developed a program philosophy and a draft site plan for the twenty-five-acre state park.

The first phase of the three-year plan, now underway, encompasses a self-guided trail on the south side of Lolo Creek, the heart of the Lewis and Clark campsite with access off Mormon Creek Road. The second phase of development will move access to an entrance off Highway 12. Approach to the main camp area will be via a trail from the north side of the Park and a footbridge over Lolo Creek. The draft site plan details trails, landscaping and interpretive stations and also includes additional possibilities for the ten-acre conservation easement. All development is contingent on adequate funding. "The key is to make it happen, do it in stages, not all at once," stated Park Director Loren Flynn.

Programs at the Park will include demonstrations, re-enactments, guided tours based on the geology botany, ecology, geography and archeology of the region. Traditional skills and crafts will be included as well as the history and culture in this area. Whenever possible the land will tell the story showing the intimacy of land and people, this at a time when society is becoming more sensitive to discovering truth in history versus myth, especially western myth such as those surrounding events like Custer's Last Stand. For ten years, beginning in 1983, archeologists combed the Custer Battlefield near Hardin, Montana, where General George Armstrong Custer and 210 men of the Seventh Cavalry were wiped out by the Sioux and Cheyenne Indians at the Battle of the Little Big Horn, June 25, 1876. Archeologists uncovered spent cartridges, bones, bullets, and various metal objects which when examined by forensic scientists and anthropologist, applying the same ballistic tests used at crime scenes, were enough evidence to form a portrait of the participants and to reconstruct the battle. Historic detectives examined eyewitness reports and drawings made by the warriors. From their findings and those of the scientists the theory emerged that the battle might really have been a short, devastating rout rather than a historic last stand. Thus, historians and the general public alike were faced with the possibility that archeological discoveries might demand a rethinking of the event.

In regard to the Travelers' Rest site, technology, its role in scientists

This view in early 2003 taken from a hill to the north of Highway 12, looking south onto Lolo Creek and the Travelers' Rest site (note the "Living Witness Tree" in the center of the picture), provides an overview of an open pasture recently purchased as a proposed entrance to the new Travelers' Rest State Park. Photo courtesy Patricia Hastings.

locating the site, and its continuing use by the Earth Observing System at the University of Montana is actively involving students as providers of data, not just recipients memorizing dates and names. Consequently, sensitivity to the land and to its preservation and stewardship hangs in the balance.

The new-found interest in Travelers' Rest will affect Lolo. Visitors to the area, especially during the Lewis and Clark Bicentennial Celebration, will impact services in the town and the surrounding area. Business interests look forward to economic betterment because of the influx of tourists which in turn will provide the impetus to improve and upgrade local features. Lolo has the advantage of location, being an important crossroads only nine miles from the major western Montana city of Missoula.

Because the Park will be self-sustaining and require only the support and not the tax dollars from the community, Lolo is in a position to enjoy the benefits without a commitment of financial responsibility. Chuck Sundstrom, president of the Travelers' Rest Chapter of the Lewis and Clark Trail Heritage Foundation which meets monthly in Lolo, is enthusiastic about the support he sees from members of his organization and from the community. From fifty members in 1995, Sundstrom asserts that "our membership has increased to over 200 in 2003." Flynn said that he is getting positive comments and feedback on the project. "The great turnout of participants at the local celebration of the opening day of the Lewis and Clark bicentennial, January 18, 2003, (a cold miserable day) and the never ending help of our volunteers tells me that locals are getting involved and we are excited about that."

The famous "winds of change over Montana" noted some years ago by historian K. Ross Toole, are, literally, blowing opportunity toward Lolo and the surrounding area but are also issuing a challenge – the challenge to nurture, nudge and incorporate this fledgling new member into the community.

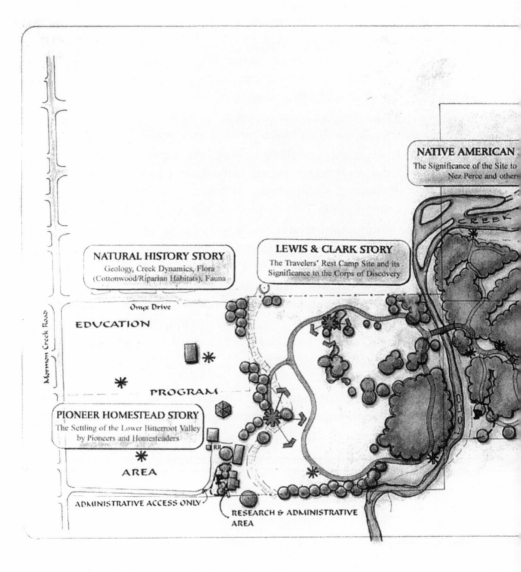

NATIVE AMERICAN
The Significance of the Site to
Nez Perce and others

NATURAL HISTORY STORY
Geology, Creek Dynamics, Flora
(Cottonwood/Riparian Habitats), Fauna

LEWIS & CLARK STORY
The Travelers' Rest Camp Site and its
Significance to the Corps of Discovery

Onyx Drive

EDUCATION

PROGRAM

PIONEER HOMESTEAD STORY
The Settling of the Lower Bitterroot Valley
by Pioneers and Homesteaders

AREA

Mormon Creek Road

CREEK

RR

ADMINISTRATIVE ACCESS ONLY

RESEARCH & ADMINISTRATIVE
AREA

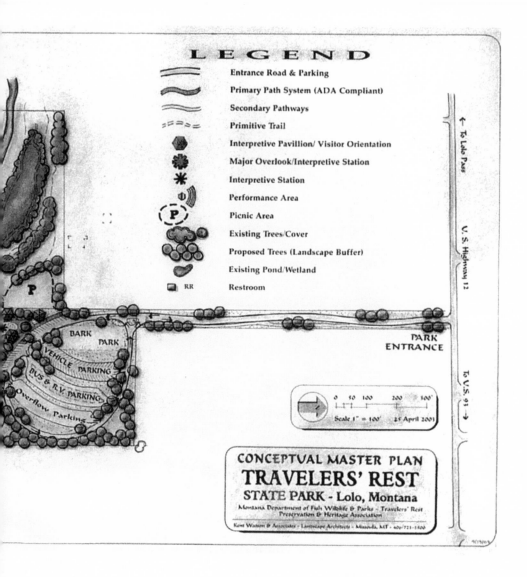

LEGEND

Entrance Road & Parking

Primary Path System (ADA Compliant)

Secondary Pathways

Primitive Trail

Interpretive Pavillion/ Visitor Orientation

Major Overlook/Interpretive Station

Interpretive Station

Performance Area

Picnic Area

Existing Trees/Cover

Proposed Trees (Landscape Buffer)

Existing Pond/Wetland

RR   Restroom

← To Lolo Pass

U. S. Highway 12

To U.S. 93 →

P

BARK PARK

VEHICLE PARKING

BUS & R.V. PARKING

Overflow Parking

PARK ENTRANCE

0   50   100   200   300'

Scale 1" = 100'   25 April 2001

CONCEPTUAL MASTER PLAN
TRAVELERS' REST
STATE PARK - Lolo, Montana
Montana Department of Fish Wildlife & Parks - Travelers' Rest
Preservation & Heritage Association
Kent Watson & Associates - Landscape Architects - Missoula, MT - 406/721-1600

EPILOGUE

Should a time capsule have allowed Thomas Jefferson and Captains Meriwether Lewis and William Clark to return after two hundred years to Travelers' Rest, they would have had to search for the "*large creek which falls in on the west,*" for their *Traveller's Rest* has meandered about three hundred paces to the north.

However, it is still "*a fine clear bould-running stream*" but now it is surrounded by houses and settlement. Fireflies and mosquitos are around, too, but not so many. Lewis would find it difficult to take his celestial observations as the stars are dimmed by the bright lights of the gas stations, restaurants and casinos on the nearby main road. Houses perch high up on the mountains, but those mountains don't look quite so formidable now. Is it because strange, frightening noisy vehicles race along the roads and then disappear into those "emmence mountains" and no one is concerned? How many days does it take them to reach Twisted Hair's camp? Men and women, boys and girls mill around the Travelers' Rest campsite wearing T-shirts imprinted with "Lewis and Clark Bicentennial," carrying cameras and taking pictures of *what – the site of the latrine*? Our time-capsule friends might ask, almost incredulously:

"*Did these men of the Twenty-first Century really dig up our latrine to find the campsite?*"

Thomas Jefferson, a man noted for a good sense of humor, might muse as he pointed to the latrine; "Ah, Meriwether, and you too, William, I certainly expected both of you to leave your footprints on history. Apparently, it is fortunate you left more than the imprints of your moccasins or the exact location of your campsite would never have been found, and all these people would have had little to celebrate here. Well done, gentlemen. Well done!"

APPENDIX

TIME-LINE FOR TRAVELERS' REST BOOK

1600's: Ancestors of today's Montana Indians arrived. Kootenai may have been the first of present day tribes.

1700's: Principal Tribes: Kalispel, Salish (Flathead), Pend Oreille, Shoshone, Gros Ventres, Nez Perce, Kootenai.

1800: Trappers are in field.

1804: Lewis and Clark Expedition leaves Camp Dubois.

1804-05: L&C Expedition winters at Fort Mandan, No. Dakota.

April. L&C Expedition leaves Mandan for unknown western lands.

September 9-11, 1805 Lewis and Clark Expedition at Travelers' Rest.

September 11-22: Over "trail to the buffalo" (Lolo Trail).

December, 1805 -March 23, 1806: Expedition winters at Fort Clatsop,

1806: June: Expedition returns over "road to buffalo" (Lolo Trail).

June 30-July 3, 1806, Lewis and Clark at Traveler's Rest.

September 23, 1806: Expedition returns to St. Louis.

1810: Fur trapper Lawrence in Lolo vicinity ("Lolo" is corruption of "Lawrence")

1812: David Thompson, employee of NorthWest Co. surveys Missoula from Mt. Jumbo.

1824: Alexander Ross trapping party passes through Hellgate Canyon.

1831: John Work leads trapping company over Lolo Trail with great difficulty.

1841: Jesuit priests establish St. Mary's Mission at Stevensville

1846: 49th parallel designated as boundary between U.S. and Canada.

Oregon wilderness ceded to United States.

1850: Major John Owens establishes trading post, Stevensville.

1853: Washington Territory formed.

Lt. John Mullan erected Cantonment Stevens in Bitterroot Valley.

1853-54: Captain Isaac Stevens directs railroad survey to Pacific.

1855: Council Grove (Hellgate) Treaty with Salish. Establishes Jocko Reservation.

1855-1862: Mullan Road built from Walla Walla, WA to Fort Benton, MT.

1860: Hellgate Trading Post built by Worden, Higgins and Woody.

Missoula County created by Washington Territory Legislature.

1862: Homesteaders Act opens up land for development.

1863: Idaho Territory created

1864: Montana Territory created

(Camels arrive in Montana)

Missoula Mills Co. built near Rattlesnake Creek, origin of city of Missoula

1865: John Delaney arrives in Lolo area.

1872: Flathead people from Bitterroot removed to Jocko Reservation in Mission Valley.

1877: Flight of the Nez Perce.

1882: Sawmills in Bitterroot Valley: beginning of timber industry.

1883: Northern Pacific RR reaches Missoula.

1883: Ravalli and Flathead Counties carved from Missoula County.

1884: Lolo School District formed.

1885: John Delaney filed for 165 acres at crossroads at Lolo.

1885. City of Missoula incorporated.

1886: Mill built at Bonner

1888: Rudimentary road exists to Lolo Hot Springs.
>   Delaney's buildings are nucleus of Lolo.

1889: Northern Pacific Railroad reaches Lolo.

1890: Beginning of development of Lolo Hot Springs.

1892: Woodman School opened.

1895: University of Montana located at Missoula.
>   Bitterroot named Montana State Flower.

1899-1900 Federal Government conducts Geodetric Survey of Lolo area.

1906: Forest Service enforce control of timber management and grazing on public lands.

1907: Research on tick fever.

1908: U.S. Forest Service regional office established at Missoula.

1910: Forest fires rage in Bitterroot Valley.
>   Business establishments grow around Lolo intersection.
>   Lumber mill built at Milltown.

1910 -1914: Apple Boom.

1919-1933: Prohibition is federal law: bootlegging in Lolo Canyon.

1959: Travelers' Rest recorded as National Historical Landmark.

1962: Lewis and Clark Highway 12 constructed along Lolo Canyon.

1963: Sign on Highway 93 erected, claiming Travelers' Rest site at mouth of Lolo Creek.

1968: Pat & Ernie Deschamps buy property on Mormon Creek in Lolo.
>   Highway 93 expands to four lanes between Lolo and Missoula.

1989: Travelers' Rest Chapter of Lewis and Clark Heritage Foundation is organized

1990's Movement develops to preserve Travelers' Rest Site,

1995: Dr. Robert Bergantino presents new evidence on location of Travelers' Rest.

1996: Travelers' Rest Chapter commission aerial infra red survey of probable Traveler's Rest site.
>   Traveling Trunk begins its journey with George Knapp and Chuck Sundstrom.

1998: Professor Robert Bergantino publishes report identifying Travelers' Rest campsite approximately 2 miles upstream from confluence of Lolo Creek and Bitterroot River, outside of the Travelers' Rest National Historic Landmark property.

1998: Travelers' Rest Chapter hires Archeologist Don Hall to make survey of land about to be developed: unearths button from 1790-1812 era.

Mr. Miller subdivides eight acres of his property which is also part of Travelers' Rest campsite.

1999: Jan. $5,500 Challenge Cost Share Grant awarded Tr. Rest Chapter from <u>National Park Service</u> for more archeological assessment and development of Lastings Legacies Conference.

Missoula Office of Planning and Grants awarded $2,900, Challenge Cost Share Grant from National Park Service to coordinate and develop Travelers' Rest Design Charette and for assistance Montana and Idaho Chapters of American Society of Landscape Architects.

HUD grant awarded to Montana Community Development Corporation (MCDC) to launch project.

National Trust of Historical Preservation lists Travelers' Rest site ninth on list of most endangered historical places in United States.

2000: Philanthropist member of National Trust for Historic Preservation purchases and preserves 4 acre barn property on Travelers' Rest site which was slated for development.

Award, $22,000 from Montana Lewis and Clark Bicentennial Commission for Missoula County's archeological research at Travelers' Rest.

Grant $500,000 to MCDC for site acquisition and operations through U.S. Forest Service.

2001: March: The Conservation Fund closes deal on 15 acre Deschamps property. Ownership transferred to Montana Department of Fish, Wildlife and Parks (FWP).

MCDC enters into agreement with FWP to develop, interpret, and manage site as a state park.

Grant $20,000, National Park Service challenge Cost Share Grant, awarded to MCDC to develop site interpretation with Salish Tribe.

Missoula County's archeology field work begins.

May: Travelers' Rest Preservation and Heritage Association incorporated and assigned all MCDC's agreements and grants associated with Travelers' Rest.

Grant $20,000 from Montana Lewis and Clark Bicentennial Commission for creation of interpretive signs, highway signs and purchase and installation of vault toilet.

2002:   Summer: Historical archaeologist Dan Hall and crew begin excavation at Travelers' Rest State Park.

July: Archaeologists identify the latrine used by Lewis and Clark and Corps of Discovery.

August: Archaeologists find a lead musket ball, a solid lead puddle, and a significant piece of charcoal in the area believed to be the Corps of Discovery central cooking and gunssmithing fire.

2003: State park offices and facility opens at Travelers' Rest site.

BIBLIOGRAPHY

Ambrose, Stephen E. *Undaunted Courage: Meriwether Lewis, Thomas Jefferson and the Opening of the American West.* New York: Simon and Schuster, 1996.

Arno, Stephen F. *Northwest Trees.* Seattle: The Mountaineers, 1977.

Bedini, Silvio A. "The Scientific Instruments of the Lewis and Clark Expedition." *Great Plain Quarterly,* Lincoln: Center for Great Plains Studies, 1984.

Bergantino, Robert. "Lewis and Clark in the Bitterroot Valley Montana 1805-1806."

---------- "Fort Mandan's Longitude Revisited." *We Proceeded On,* vol. 27, no. 4 (Nov.2001).

Bicentennial Committee Bonner School. *A Grass Roots Tribute; The Study of Bonner, Montana.* Missoula: Gateway Printing, 1976.

Burk, Mary K. & Bruce T. Burk. *Dusty Trails up Lolo Creek: The Don Babcock Collection A Pictorial Journey Through the Heart of the Bitterroot Mountains.* Lolo, MT.: Laughing Stock Press, 2002.

Burroughs, Raymond Darwin, ed. *The National History of the Lewis and Clark Expedition.* East Lansing: Michigan State University Press, 1995.

Campbell, Charles V. *Guidebook for Routes Followed by Lewis and Clark Across the Rocky Mountains in 1805-06.* Missoula: Missoula Travelers Rest Chapter of the Lewis and Clark Trail Heritage Foundation, 1994.

Constant, Constantine. *Earth Science Workbook.* New York: Amsco School Publications. Inc. 1972.

Coues, Elliot, ed. *History of the Expedition Under the Command of Lewis and Clark.* New York: Dover Publications, reprint three volumes, 1963.

Cutright, Paul Russell. *Lewis and Clark: Pioneering Naturalists.* Lincoln: University of Nebraska Press. 1969.

-------- "Meriwether Lewis: Naturalist." Portland: *The Oregon Historical Quarterly,* 1969.

Cheney, Roberta Carkeet. *Names on the Face of Montana.* Missoula: Mountain Press Publishing Co., 1983.

Dattilio, Daniel J. ed. Butcher, Russell D. *Fort Clatsop: The Story Behind the Scenery.* Las Vegas: K.C. Publications, Inc., 1996.

DeVoto, Bernard. *The Course of Empire.* Cambridge: The Riverside Press, 1952.

-------- ed. *The Journals of Lewis and Clark.* Boston: Houghton, Mifflin Co. Riverside Press Cambridge, 1953.

Discovery Writers. *Lewis and Clark in the Bitterroot.* Stevensville, MT.: Stoneydale Press, 1998.

Driver, Harold E. *Indians of North America.* Chicago: University of Chicago Press, 1961.

Dougherty, Michael & Heidi. *The Ultimate Montana Atlas and Travel Encyclopedia.* Bozeman: Ultimate Press, 2001.

Duncan, Dayton & Burns, Ken. *Lewis and Clark, the Journey of the Corps of Discovery.* New York: Alfred A. Knopf, 1997.

Fanslow, Julie. *The Travelers Guide to the Lewis and Clark Trail.* Helena: Falcon Press, Inc. 1994.

Fazio, James R. *Across the Snowy Ranges: The Lewis and Clark Expedition in Idaho and Montana.* Moscow, Id.: Woodland Press, 2001.

Federal Workers Project of Works Project Administration. *The WPA Guide to 1930's Montana.* Tucson: University of Arizona Press, 1939.

Fifer, Barbara & Soderberg, Vicki. *Along the Trail with Lewis and Clark.* Great Falls: Montana Magazine, 1998.

Geist, Valerius. *Mule Deer Country.* Northwood Press, Inc. 1990.

Gibbons, Loren M. "All Them Horses and One Poor Mule." *We Proceeded On* (August, 2002).

Griggs. Jack. *All the Birds of North America.* New York: Harper Perennial, 1997.

Haines, Francis. *The Nez Perces, Tribesmen of the Columbia Plateau.* Norman: University of Oklahoma Press, 1955.

Hendrickson, Berg & Laughy, Linwood. *Clearwater Country! The Traveler's Historical and   Recreational Guide Lewiston Idaho, Missoula, Montana, Kooskia, Idaho.* Mountain Meadow Press, 1990.

Howes, Kathi. *The Nez Perce.* Florida: Vero Beach: Rourke Publications, Inc.

Jackson, Donald, ed. *Letters of the Lewis and Clark Expedition, with Related Documents: 1783-1854.* 2nd ed. Urbana: University of Illinois Press, 1978.

James, Caroline. *Nez Perce Women in Transition* 1877-1990. Moscow: University of Idaho Press, 1996.

Josephy, Alvin M. Jr. *The Nez Perce Indians and the Opening of the Northwest.* Lincoln and London: University of Nebraska Press, 1965.

---------- *Chief Joseph's People and Their War.* Yellowstone Library and Museum Association. 1964.

----------"The Last Stand of Chief Joseph." *American Heritage.* American Heritage Publishing Co. Inc., Vol. IX, No. 4. (Feb. 1958).

Knapp, George. "The Search for Lolo." *Westward Barriers: Newsletter of Travelers' Rest Chapter of the Lewis and Clark Trail Heritage Foundation* vol. 2003, no. 3 (March).

Keating, Linnea. Pamphlet, *Brief History of Public Works Programs on the Clearwater National Forest: 1933-1943.* Orofino, Idaho: Clearwater National Forest District, June 1983.

Koebel, Lenora. *Missoula, the Way it Was: A Portrait of the Early Western Town.* Missoula: Gateway Inc. & Lito, 1972.

Lackschewitz, Klaus. "Vascular Plants of West-Central Montana*"-Identification*

Guidebook. Missoula: U.S. Forest Service, 1986.

Landen, Dan and Pinkham, Allen. *Salmon and his People, Fish and Fishing in Nez Perce Culture*. Lewiston, Idaho: Confluence Press, 1999.

Laubin, Reginald and Gladys. *The Indian Tipi*. New York: University of Oklahoma Press, 1957.

Lawrence, Russ. *Montana's Bitterroot Valley: Just Short of Paradise*. Stevensville: Stoneydale Press, 1999.

Little, Elbert L., Jr., *Forest Trees of the United States and Canada, and How to Identify Them*. Washington, DC: United States Department of Agriculture, 1978.

Lolo Women's Club. *Lolo Creek Reflections*. Stevensville: Stoneydale Press. 1999.

MacGregor, Carol Lynn, ed. *The Journals of Patrick Gass, Member of the Lewis and Clark Expedition*. Missoula: Mountain Press Publishing Company, 1997.

McRae, W.C. and Jewell, Judy. *Montana Handbook*. California, Chico: Moon Publications, Inc. 1999.

McWhorter, L.V. *Wolf: His Own Story*. Caldwell, Idaho: The Caxon Printers, Ltd., 1948.

----------*Hear Me My Chiefs!* Caldwell, Idaho: The Caxton Printers, Ltd., 1952.

Merrell, Carolynne. "Culturally Peeled Tree Inventory Along the Historic Lolo Trail." *Clearwater National Forest Resport, document No. 1443-1A 9000-94-027,* 1998.

----------and James Clark. "Peeled Lodgepole Pine: A disappearing Culture Resource and Archeological Record." *Northwest Anthropoligical Research Notes*. Vol. 35,1, 2001.

Moore, Bud. *The Lochsa Story*. Missoula: Mountain Press Publishing Co., 1996.

Moore, Robert J., Jr., *Lewis & Clark: Tailor Made: Trail Worn*. Helena: Farcountry Press, 2003.

Moulton, Gary, ed. *The Journals of the Lewis and Clark Expedition*. Lincoln: University of Nebraska, 1983-97..

Nabokov, Peter and Easton, Robert. *Native American Architecture*. New York and Oxford: Oxford University Press, 1989.

Namowitz, Samuel N. and Stone, Donald B. *Earth's Science: Teacher's Annotated Edition*. New York: American Book Co. Litton Educational Publications, Inc. 1978.

O'Connor, Jack. "The Big Game Animals of North America." *Outdoor Life*. New York: E.P. Dutton & Co. Inc. 1961.

Peterson, Roger Tory. *Peterson Field Guides: Western Birds*. Boston: Houghton Mifflin Co., 1990.

Quaife, Milo, ed. *The Journals of Meriwether Lewis and Sergeant John Ordway*. Madison: The State Historical Society of Wisconsin, 1916.

Ritter, Sharon A. *Lewis and Clark's Mountain Wilds*. Moscow: University of Idaho Press, 2002.

Ronda, James P. *Lewis and Clark Among the Indians.* Lincoln: University of Nebraska Press, 1984.

--------ed. *Voyages of Discovery.* Helena: Montana Historical Society Press, 1998. "The Core of Discovery." *We Proceeded On,* Feb. 1999.

Rue, Leonard Lee III. *Pictorial Guide of the Mammals of North America.* New York: Thomas Y. Crowell Company, 1967.

"Rush, Benjamin". *Encyclopedia Britannica.* Vol. 16, 1982.

Schneider, Bill. *The Flight of the Nez Perce.* Helena: Falcon Press, 1992.

Space, Ralph. *The Lolo Trail: A History of Events Connected with the Lolo Trail Since Lewis and Clark.* Lewiston: Idaho Printcraft Printing, 1984.

Spritzer, Don. *Roadside History of Montana.* Missoula: Mountain Press, 1999.

Starr, Eileen. "Celestial Navigation Basics," *We Proceeded On.,* vol. 27 no. 4. (Nov. 2001)

Steuben, Frederick William Baron von. *Baron von Steuben's Revolutionary War Drill Manual.* New York: Dover Publications Inc. 1794.

Stevensville Historical Society. *Montana Genesis.* Missoula: Mountain Press, 1971.

Stone, Arthur L. *Following Old Trails.* Missoula: Pictorial Histories Publishing Co., Inc. 1996.

Swan, Kenneth D. *Splendid Was the Trail.* Missoula: Sweetgrass Books, 1993.

Thorp, Daniel. *Lewis & Clark, An American Journey.* Metro Books, an imprint of Freedman Fairfax Publishers, 1998.

Thwaites, Reuben G.,ed. *Original Journals of the Lewis and Clark Expedition.* New York: Dodd and Mead and Company, 1904.

Tirrell, Norma. *Montana.* Oakland: Compass American Guides, Inc. 1991.

Toole, K. Ross. *Montana: An Uncommon Land.* Norman: University of Oklahoma Press. 1959.

Thwaites, Reuben G., ed. *Original Journals of the Lewis and Clark Expedition 1805-1806.* New York: Dodd and Mead and Co., 1904-05.

Travelers' Rest Preservation and Heritage Association www.travelersrest.org

Wheeler, Olin A. *The Trail of Lewis and Clark, 1804-1806.* New York: G.P. Putnam and Sons, 1916. Vol. 2.

Wissler, Clark. *Indians of the United States.* New York: Doubleday Anchor Books, 1966.

Wright, William H. *The Grizzly Bear: The Narrative of a Hunter-Naturalist.* New York: Charles Scribner & Sons, 1910.

GLOSSARY

Bitterroot River: names for
        Spitlem seukm (Salish-Flathead)
        Flathead (Lewis and Clark)
        Clark's River (Lewis)
        St. Mary's (Pierre DeSmet S. J.)

Clark Fork River: names for
        Valley Plain River: east fork of Bitterroot river.
        Hellgate River
        Missoula River

Choppunish: Captain Clark's name for the Nez Perce people.

Cokahlarishkit River: (Nez Perce) river of the "road to the buffalo," the present-day "Big Blackfoot River."

Flathead: Misnomer for Salish Indians.

Glade Creek: (Idaho) Pack Creek, east of Lolo Pass.

Hote Spring: Lolo Hot Springs.

Janey: Captain Clark's name for Sacajawea.

Khusahna (Ku-sey-ne-ess-kit) (Nez Perce): "Buffalo Trail."

Kooskooskee: Clearwater River.

Lolo: Indian word meaning "muddy water."

Oot-la-shoots: a band of Tushepa or Salish Indians.

Packer Meadows: Lower End of Pack Creek.

Pahkees: (Nez Perce) enemy.

Pomp: Captain Clark's name for Jean Baptiste Charbonneau, Sacajawea's son.

Quawmash: camas plant root plant used by Indians for food.

Quawmash Flats: Wieppe Prairie

Quawmash Glades: Packer Meadows

Roche Jaune (French): Yellowstone River.

Shalees: (Nez Perce) Salish Indians

Snakes: another name for Shoshone Indians.

Snowey Mountain: Wendover Ridge

So ya pos: (Nez Perce) "white men."

Spitlem suelken: (Salish)"Water of the Bitterroot," (Bitterroot River)

Spitlemen: (Salish) "Place of the Bitterroot" (Bitterroot Valley) also
                "Bitterroot plant"

Travellers Rest: present day "Lolo Creek."

Tumsumlech: (Salish) "No salmon," Lolo Creek.

INDEX

A
Ambrose, Stephen, 28, 123, 148
Anaconda, 151
Anaconda Copper Mining Co., 151
Archeological Excavations, 41
Articles of War, 145
B
Barton, Dr. Benjamin Smith, 74
Bear, black, grizzly 86-90
Beaverhead River, 115
Belt Creek, 114
Bergantino, Dr. Robert, 40, 42, 134
Big Hole River, 157
Big Hole Valley, 19, 20, 35, 39
Big Horn, battle of, 155, 156,
Billings, 41
Bitterroot, plant 78,80
Bitterroot Mountains, 9, 14, 17, 20, 30, 31, 39, 46, 51, 52, 53, 59, 61, 69, 76, 80, 91, 93, 107, 109, 138, 142
Bitterroot River,10, 18, 49, 80, 115, 127, 157
Bitterroot Valley, 15, 21, 32, 35, 41, 43, 54, 80, 83, 85,119, 128, 155, 157, 164
Blackfeet, 139
Blackfoot River, 11, 34
Bonner, 150
Bozeman Pass, 36
Butte, 151
C
Camas, 77, 78
Cameahwait, 20, 149
Camp Creek, 10, 21
Camp Decision, 114
Camp Disappointment, 35
Camp Fortunate,115
Camp Wood (Dubois)131, 137
Celestial Readings, 128, 133
Charbonneau, Jean Baptiste, 37, 61, 137 (see Pomp)
Charbonneau, Toussiant, 22, 36, 37, 114, 145
Charlo, Chief, 22
Choppunish, 68, 82, 95
Cheyenne Indians, 166
Chief Joseph, 154, 155, 156, 157
Chief Looking Glass, 156

Civilian Conservation Corps, 153, 162, 163
Clark Canyon, 35,
Clark Fork Canyon, 149
Clark Fork River, 32, 85, 113, 114, 149
Clark's Nutcracker, 83
Clark's River, 24, 25, 32, 40, 75, 77
Clark, William, 28, 31, 32, 33, 34, 35, 36, 39, 40, 47, 55, 56, 58, 59, 62, 63, 65, 66, 67, 68, 71, 73, 81, 82, 85, 86, 96, 109, 110, 115, 130, 131, 139,141, 142, 145, 147, 149, 171
Clearwater National Forest, 148, 152, 163
Clearwater Railroad, 117
Clearwater River, 27, 51, 58, 62, 63, 64, 65, 67, 68, 69, 82, 90, 91, 92, 94, 153, 155, 159
Clinton, William Jefferson, 159
Colt Killed Creek, 57, 69, 140, 141
Colter, John 26, 37, 65, 67, 92
Columbia Basin: 17, 52 and Plateau 107, 141
Columbia River: 17, 24, 26, 28 and Plains 34, 37, 53, 58, 63, 64, 94, 95
Colville Reservation, 157
Corps of Discovery, 56, 60, 62, 63, 64, 65, 66, 70, 71, 93, 138, 145, 154, 157, 159, 164
Cous, root, 84
Crow Indians, 36, 156, 157, 158
Cruzette, Pierre, 28, 34, 107
Custer, George Armstrong, 155, 166
Cut Bank Creek, 35
D
Dalles, 28, 31
Deer, (Whitetail and Mule), 71, 86, 88
Delaney, John, 119
Dendorchronology, 1143
Deschamps, Pat and Ernie, 121, 122, 123, 123
Deschamps, Cathy, 123
DeVoto, Bernard, 25
Discovery Writers, 9, 11
Douglas, David, 76
Drouillard, George (Drewyer), 22, 35, 65, 66, 67, 68, 114, 139
F
Fazio, James, 32, 148
Field, Joseph, 32, 35, 66, 67, 68, 71, 114
Field, Reuben, 32, 35, 63, 66, 67, 68, 84, 114
Flathead River, 24, 26, 74, 75
Flathead Indians, 22, 68, 149
Floyd, Charles, 37
Flynn, Loren, 165, 167
Fort Clatsop, 29, 30, 112

Fort Fizzle, 157
Fort Mandan, 19, 111, 112, 115, 131
Fort Missoula, 155, 162
Franklin, Benjamin, 45
Frazer, Robert (Frazier) 62, 67, 114
Fritz, Harry, 42
G
Gass, Patrick, 20, 27, 31, 32, 34, 56, 58, 62, 63, 67, 85, 109, 110, 114
Gates of the Mountains, 19
Gibbons Pass, 20, 115, 157
Gibson, George, 36
Glade Creek, 77, 147-149
Glade Meadows (Idaho), 71
Goodrich, Silas, 32, 47, 114
Gorski, Margaret, 161
Grant Creek, 33, 85, 113
Grave Creek, 55, 71
Great Falls, 19, 32, 33, 36, 150, 151
Grouse (Franklin and Spruce), 61, 62, 82
H
Hall, Daniel, 41, 47, 48
Hellgate Canyon, 33, 34, 149, 150
Hellgate River, 32
Henry, Hugh, 115
Herbaceous Plants, 77-80
Hidatsa Indians, 22
Higgins, Christopher, 149
Howard, General Oliver, 156
Holt, (Bill and Ramona), 41
Hot Springs, 30
Hungry Creek, 61, 62, 65, 66, 142
I
Indian Post Office, 141, 158
J
Jefferson, River, 115, 128
Jefferson, Thomas, 13, 14, 17, 18, 45, 53, 73, 108, 111, 141
K
Kamiah Ranger Station, 153
Knapp, George, 124, 126
Kootenai Indians, 39, 153
Koo Koo Ski River 57
Kooskia Ranger Station, 143, 153
L
Labiche, Francois, 22
Latrine, 41, 47, 49,162
Lawrence, 117

Lead, 145, 147

LePage, Jean Baptiste, 62, 65

Lemhi, 65, 82

Lewis and Clark, 29, 40, 42, 46, 48, 84, 86, 94, 111, 128,142, 143, 159

Lewis and Clark Expedition, 52, 56, 85, 93, 98, 124, 126, 139,152

Lewis and Clark Trail Heritage Foundation, 14, 46, 121, 123, 148

Lewis and Clark National Trail 161, 165

Lewis, Meriwether, 10, 29, 30, 31, 32, 33, 34, 35, 39, 41, 45, 47, 54, 56, 57, 62, 63, 65, 66, 67, 68, 69, 70, 74, 76, 77, 80, 84, 96, 98, 108, 109, 110, 113, 114, 115, 122, 123, 130, 131, 138, 139,147, 151, 171

Lewis' Woodpecker, 83

Living Witness Tree 72, 74

Lochsa, River, 57, 58, 61, 69, 70, 71, 141, 153

Lolo, 10, 40, 120, 167

Lolo Creek, 10, 29, 30, 31, 32, 33, 34, 35, 39, 41, 45, 47, 51, 53, 56, 57, 62, 63, 66, 68, 75,119,145, 165

Lolo Creek Canyon, Idaho, 64, 66, 71

Lolo Hot Springs, 32, 55, 56, 70, 118, 152,

Lolo Motorway, 153

Lolo National Forest, 161

Lolo Pass Visitor Center 147, 152,162

Lolo Road, 161

Lolo Trail, 10, 39, 51, 52, 53, 55, 56, 62, 141, 142, 158, 164

Lolo Trail Pass, 53, 57, 69, 91, 138

Longitude and Latitude,128, 134

Lou Lou Fork, 25

Lost Trail Pass, 10, 53

M

Mandan Village,13, 18, 36, 37, 137

Marias River, 9, 10, 35, 40, 84, 111, 114, 139

McNeal, Hugh, 32, 47, 114

Medicine chest, 44

Medicine River, 114

Mercury, 41, 44, 46, 47, 130

Mercury vapor analyzer, 48, 130

Merrell, Carolynne, 143, 147, 148

Menzies, Archibald, 76

Milltown, 150

Minnetarees, 33, 147

Missoula, 33, 34, 36, 117,147, 150, 153, 155, and Garden City, 162

Missoula County, 150

Missoula Mills Co., 150

Missouri River, 18, 30, 34, 40, 76, 84, 110

Moore, Bud, 161

Mormon Creek Road, 121, 123, 145

Mullan, John, 149,118

Mullan Road, 149
N
Native American, 17, 27, 28, 29, 33, 35, 42, 51, 81, 140, 145, 153, 162
National Park Service, 159
Nee Mee Poo Trail, 20, 65, 70, 94. 95, 98, 108, 157
Nez Perce, 23, 27, 30, 32, 33, 34, 35, 39, 42, 46, 47, 51, 53, 56, 58, 62, 64, 65, 66, 67, 69, 77, 91, 93, 94, 95, 96, 97, 98, 110, 136, 138, 141, 143, 145, 146, 153, 154, 155, 156, 157, 164, 165
Nez Perce Trail, 59, 71, 150, 157, 158
Northwest Passage, 13, 14, 39, 111
Northern Pacific Railway, 57, 118,150
O
Octant, 128-133
Old Dutch Lady, 160
Old Toby, 20, 24, 27, 28, 39, 56, 58, 71, 93, 94, 138, 141
Ootlashoot Indians, 22, 71
Ordway, John, 20, 22, 24, 34, 35, 54, 60, 91, 114, 115
Owens, Major John, 126
P
Pacific Ocean, 13, 17, 52
Pacific Coast, 39
Packer Meadows, 57, 77, 91, 152, 162, 163
Passenger pigeon, 84
Pattee, David, 150
Peeled trees, 52, 58, 65, 141
Pend d'Oreille, 39
Philadelphia, 45, 123
P.I.T. (Pastport in Time), 142
Plants: flora, 74-80
Plum Creek Timber Co., 161
Pomp, (also see Jean Baptiste Charbonneau) 61, 114, 115
Pompey's Pillar, 15, 36, 41, 49, 114, 139
Potts, John, 47, 66
Powell Ranger Station, 140, 158
Pryor, Nathaniel, 36
Q
Quamash, 57, 95
R
Rattlesnake Creek, 149, 150
Red Grizzly Bear, Chief, 108
Ronda, James, 23
Road to the Buffalo, 26, 34, 39, 94
Road to the Missouri, 20
Rochejhone, (see Yellowstone River)
Rocky Mountains, 31, 54, 85, 86, 111
Rocky Mountain Spotted Fever, 119

Ross' Hole, 20, 22, 39, 115, 138, 157
Rush, Dr. Benjamin, 45, 46
Rush's pills, 46, 47
S
Sacajawea, 19, 27, 28, 29, 32, 36, 61, 68, 114, 136, 159
Saint Charles, 87
Saint Louis, 37, 65, 115
Saint Mary's Mission, 127
Salish Indians, 10, 22, 23, 31, 33, 39, 51, 53, 58, 77, 80, 126, 127, 141, 153
Salmon River, 10, 20, 54, 58
Scarred trees (also see peeled trees), 142
Seaman, 31, 33, 151
Sextant, 128-133
Shannon, George, 65, 67
Sherman Peak, 61, 62, 68
Shields, John, 138, 145
Shoshone Indians, 19, 22, 23, 26, 80, 93, 137
Shrubs, 76, 77
Sigars, Denny, 148
Sink, (also see latrine), 49, 145
Sioux Indians, 166
Snake River, 64, 95
Sohon, Gustav, 25
Squirrels: Columbian and Red, 85, 86
Steuben, Baron Frederick William von, 145
Stevens, Isaac, 154
Stevensville, 24, 127, 157
Stimson Lumber Company, 151
Sundstrom, Chuck, 15, 125, 126, 167
Swanzey, Dr. Eugene, 20, 21, 24
Sweatlodge, 134-136
T
Tents, 145, 146, 147, 162
Teton Sioux, 37, 115
Three Forks, 19, 34, 35
Thompson, John, 32, 114
Toole, K. Ross, 25, 120, 167
Traveling Trunk, 42, 46, 124, 125, 126
Travelers' Rest, 9, 10, 14, 17, 18, 24, 25, 30, 35, 39, 40, 41, 48, 49, 54, 67, 69, 71, 72, 76, 78, 83, 84, 85, 86, 89, 90, 93, 109, 110, 112, 115, 122, 124, 126, 138, 139, 142, 145, 157, 159, 160, 161, 164, 165, 166, 167, 168, 171
Trees, 74-76, 141-143
TRHPA (Travelers' Rest Preservation and Heritage Association), 26
Tushapa Indians, 22
Twisted Hair, 28, 63, 64, 171
Two Medicine, 35

U
University of Montana, 34, 39, 150
United States Army, 145, 162
United States Forest Service, 23, 141, 142, 148, 153, 159, 161, 162
V
Valley Plain River, 25
Vigilantes, 150
W
Walla Walla Indians, 31
Weippe Prairie, 27, 51, 62, 64, 67, 71, 77, 80, 85, 94, 95, 97, 138, 154
Weiser, Peter, 67
Wendover Ridge, 27, 59, 70
Werner, William, 32, 114
White Bear Portage Camp, 34, 114, 115
Whitebird, Chief, 155, 156
Whitehouse, Joseph, 23, 24, 54, 55, 56, 58, 60, 67, 76, 95, 138, 142
Woodman Creek, 54
Woody, Frank, 149
Worden, Francis, 149
Work, John, 117
Wyakin, 89
Y
Yellowstone River, 9, 34, 36, 49, 110, 111, 113, 114, 115, 139
York, 20, 28, 159

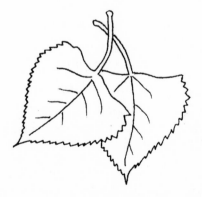

Note From the Publisher:

With the burgeoning interest in our heritage regarding the Lewis & Clark Expedition's epic journey, and the Travelers' Rest story in particular as part of that awesome saga, we thought you might like to know of a way that you can help develop and maintain this incredible place. Hence, The Discovery Writers and Stoneydale Press call your attention to the following item:

TRAVELERS' REST
PRESERVATION AND HERITAGE ASSOCIATION

The Travelers' Rest Preservation and Heritage Association is the nonprofit organization charged with managing, developing, and interpreting the Park for the State of Montana. Its programs will provide a legacy of enjoyment and learning for future generations. However, the association depends on financial support from its friends.

To make a donation, send it to:

Travelers' Rest Preservation and Heritage Association
P.O. Box 995
Lolo, MT 59847
(Phone: 406-273-4253)
or
To donate on line with credit card go to www.travelersrest.org.